The
Secret Method
for
Growing Younger

THE SECRET METHOD FOR GROWING YOUNGER

A STEP-BY-STEP GUIDE BASED ON THE LAW OF ATTRACTION

ELLEN WOOD

To Erica
Joy! Joy! Joy!
Ellen

StarHouse Creations
Questa, New Mexico

Star House Creations, PO Box 890, Questa, NM 87556

Excerpt from "A Romp Through the Quantum Field" with Dr. Bruce Lipton by Meryl Ann Butler reprinted with permission of Awareness Magazine.

Excerpt from "Living Long and Prospering" by Ulysses Torassa appeared in the June 3, 2001 edition of the San Francisco Chronicle and is used with permission.

Excerpt from the book *Creative Visualization* © Copyright 2002 by Shakti Gawain, reprinted with permission of New World Library, Novato, CA. www.newworldlibrary.com

Excerpt from "Mind Over Genes: The New Biology" by Dr. Bruce Lipton, reprinted with permission. Visit www.brucelipton.com for further information.

Excerpt from *Ask and It Is Given* © Copyright 2004 by Esther and Jerry Hicks, reprinted with permission of Hay House, Inc., Carlsbad, CA.

Excerpts from *Life and Teaching of the Masters of the Far East, vol. 1* © Copyright 1964 by Baird T. Spalding, reprinted with permission of DeVorss & Co., Marina del Rey, CA.

Excerpt from *Grow Younger, Live Longer* © Copyright 2001 by Deepak Chopra, M.D. and David Simon, M.D., Harmony Press, New York.

Excerpt from *Social Intelligence* © Copyright 2006 by Daniel Goleman, Random House, New York.

Excerpt from *The Isaiah Effect* © Copyright 2000 by Gregg Braden, Three Rivers Press, New York.

Excerpt from *A Return to Love* © Copyright 1992 by Marianne Williamson, reprinted by permission of HarperCollins, New York.

Excerpt from "More Messages in Water: The Spirit of Ma'at interviews, Dr. Masaru Emoto" by Reiko Myamoto Dewey, Spirit of Ma'at Magazine.

FIRST EDITION
Design by Jeff Spicer

ISBN-10 0-9794045-0-9
ISBN-13 978-0-9794045-0-4

For Peter, Summer, Winton and Harper,
and for Bob Swanick

TABLE OF CONTENTS

Foreword by Dr. C. Norman Shealy

Introduction

Chapter 1: The Law of Attraction   1

Chapter 2: Evolution of This Program   11

Chapter 3: Examining Your Perceptions of Old Age   21

Chapter 4: Changing Focus: The 30-Second Grow
            Younger Method™   35

Chapter 5: Powerful Transformation Tools: Youthfulness
            Collage and The Creation Planner™   53

Chapter 6: Six Habits to Guarantee Your Success   77

Chapter 7: Why Growing Younger Matters   93

Recommended Reading   104

Acknowledgements

About the Author

FOREWORD

The Power of Positive Thinking has been around for half a century but the principles were discovered and elaborated at least a century ago. Emil Coue, the famous French pharmacist, is reported to have cured over 10,000 people with his famous statement "Every day, in every way, I am getting better and better." Interestingly, he was attacked by the American Medical Association when he toured the United States. Napoleon Hill's *Think and Grow Rich* is still the classic in the world of wealth. And, of course, Dale Carnegie's reputation and wealth were accomplished with the same principles.

In the field of health, J. H. Schultz demonstrated as early as 1932 that 80 percent of individuals could cure themselves of stress illnesses (and all illnesses are stress induced!) with Autogenic Training. By 1969 there were 2,600 scientific articles on the benefits of Autogenic Training. Olympic athletes, businesspeople and students all improved their performance when they used the simple autogenic phrases. Schultz believed that these powerful repetitions retrained and rebalanced the central homeostatic control system of the brain.

Most recently *The Secret* has caught the attention of millions and been featured on *Oprah*. *The Secret* is really no secret at all. The power of positive thinking and its resultant positive attraction has been studied and emphasized by leaders in every field. In the 1950s Ambrose Worrall, a well-known spiritual healer working with his wife Olga for thirty-five years at Mount Washington United Methodist Church in Baltimore, wrote one of my favorite booklets, "Essay on Prayer". The essence of it is that every thought is a prayer. Thinking sets in motion spiritual forces to bring about changes in environment, body, hopes and despairs.

Ellen Wood has integrated this century of positive thinking and its effect upon health to the next level – its power not only to retard aging but to reverse it! We are what we think. Think boldly and think young! The only thing you have to lose is age.

C. Norman Shealy, M.D., Ph.D.
President, Holos University Graduate Seminary
Founding President of American Holistic Medical Association
Author of LIFE BEYOND 100—SECRETS OF THE
FOUNTAIN OF YOUTH

INTRODUCTION

"Who are *you*?" my mother asked me again. It was the third time in twenty minutes, and a regular ritual during my visits to the nursing home in the last months of her life in 1994.

I knew it was useless, but I wanted to beg her to remember me. *Remember how close we were, Mom? When I was little, I sat on your bed and listened to your marvelous stories of miracles. I used to help you feed the homeless when the smell of your homemade bread wafted out our back door and made them come knocking. You curled my hair and taught me how to take care of my skin and wear makeup, and you were always there for me, even when my misbehaviors broke your heart. Nothing I did could ever deter you from loving me.*

My sister was my mother's primary caregiver in her last years and I have no doubt her devotion helped Mom live longer than she would have otherwise. But the ravages of Alzheimer's eventually extinguished a life that had shown little mental or physical capacity for more than three years.

Alzheimer's. They say it's hereditary.

I remember thinking: is that what is going to happen to me? Will I get Alzheimer's too? Even if I manage to avoid that dreaded disease, will I deteriorate mentally and physically in other ways with age? Will I begin to lose strength and flexibility as my joints creak and my bones thin? Will I become set in my ways and inflexible in my thinking? Will I have to stay cooped up in the house, afraid of slipping and tripping? As I advance in years, will my mind become less clear, less sharp, until I can't remember what day it is, who my children are, or even who I am?

Who *am* I? My mother's last words to me were more profound than I realized at the time. It wasn't until ten years later that I became conscious that I have a choice about who I am going to be in my later years. Let me say that once more. It's a simple, quiet declaration, but one that has made a world of difference to me:

I choose how I will spend the rest of my life.

All my life I've searched and studied and applied the ancient secrets for creating the life I want. Why not, I realized, use that same wisdom to turn my back on Alzheimer's and develop a program for a clear mind and strong body for the rest of my life?

And so, rather than focusing on what I would *not* be able to do, or have, or be – instead of focusing on progressive deterioration and the losses and fears we expect as we accumulate birthdays, I choose to concentrate on what I want my life to be. I use the Law of Attraction and other age-reversing techniques to give me vitality, stamina, flexibility, love, creativity, exuberance, a sharp mind and a strong body.

Following this conscious-living path and using the Law of Attraction has brought me all the things I most dearly cherish: inner peace, joy, loving family relationships and friendships, and abundance of all kinds. Sure, I have a bad day every now and then, but even on those days I can't help but be grateful for the love and joy and youthful energy in my life.

It is my passion to share my youthfulness approach with you. The information contained in *The Secret Method for Growing Younger* will prepare your mind to accept and claim the power to reverse aging. This power is yours already! It is simply a matter of knowing how to access it. For that, I offer this method.

Dear reader, I promise that if you faithfully practice these techniques, you will attract all the advantages of youthfulness and your life will become joyful, just as mine is. I wish you enormous success and encourage you to share your experiences, results, comments or questions with our online community at *www.howtogrowyounger.com*.

Joy and Blessings,
Ellen Wood

THE
LAW
OF
ATTRACTION

"Neuroscience has discovered that our brain's very design makes it sociable, inexorably drawn into an intimate brain-to-brain linkup whenever we engage with another person. That neural bridge lets us affect the brain—and so the body—of everyone we interact with, just as they do us."

Daniel Goleman, *Social Intelligence:
The New Science of Human Relationships*

This is an exciting time to be alive. The science of aging has progressed rapidly in recent years. The technology necessary for more youthful bodies and life extension beyond one hundred makes exponential progress every day. Nanotechnologies are opening new opportunities to increase our lifespan and cure many illnesses. Think about what will be possible ten ... twenty ... thirty years from now. Will you be alive, alert, and prepared to accept all that the new technologies have to offer? By following the steps in this book, you will be.

In these pages you will learn that you have the power to choose strength over frailty, freedom over dependence, sexual vibrancy over isolating infirmity. It's a matter of taking control of the process, of making conscious choices – choices that can have astonishing results. You can do it without pain, without injections, without expense, without a single dreadful-tasting thing to consume. The only significant side effect you might experience is an increase in spontaneous joy.

Do you wish you had more energy? Would you like it if your mind were more agile, your body stronger and more flexible, your sex life more rewarding, your relationships more balanced and intimate? Do you want more joy, more exuberance, more libido, more compassion?

You have the power to claim all that, and more. Youthfulness isn't something bestowed upon you from outside; it's a secret strength tucked inside that gets buried over time by the buffeting winds of stress and experience, worry, exposure, and inaccurate expectation. And in the same way that we left our youth behind, we can, step-by-step uncover the source of youthfulness that has always been present at our core. This time, however, we are wiser, stronger, and steadier, and the old saying that "youth is wasted on the young" need no longer apply.

What does it mean to age?

What fixed biological processes ordain the ways our bodies will change in later years? How much of what we think about growing older is socially generated? Gerontologists, social scientists, and the best literary minds have all grappled with these questions and the annals of research stress the amazing variety of ways that humans age, both as individual biological creatures and as members of a wider culture. **Still, the image of the vibrant, sexy, capable older person takes a distant back seat to society's picture of the wrinkled, dependent elderly.**

It's clear that aging affects different people in different ways. You might know someone who puts in full days daredevil skiing in his late sixties (I do!), and another who, at forty-eight, feels that the best days of her life are a distant memory.

One thing is certain: with the average age of Americans rising steadily and advancing technology making it possible to live longer, our picture of the mature man or woman is undergoing fundamental change. There's a revolution happening, a movement made up of people like you and me who don't believe we're meant to age the way our parents did. We believe that we can grow younger consciously – and, conscious of our power, put it to good use. By practicing the steps in *The Secret Method for Growing Younger*, we can increase the joy quotient in our own lives and the lives of those around us.

The Secret Universal Law

It's not just cutting-edge science that promises exciting changes in the way we age. There's a secret afoot. This secret is called the Law of Attraction. The enlightened masters have known about it since ancient times. The truth is, by aligning ourselves with this fundamental law of how the universe works, it's possible to reverse the losses we used to think came naturally with growing older.

Science is catching on to the way our thoughts – and even the thoughts of those who surround us – influence our health and well-being. In his book *Social Intelligence*, Daniel Goleman writes about the latest findings in biology and brain science. He tells us about research that shows how connected we are, brain to brain, with those around us, and how those interactions can have actual physical consequences. We can "catch" another person's emotions, just like a cold or love fever. And those emotional reactions assert a biological influence by launching surges of hormones that can harm or improve our bodies.

You and I already know through experience that bad relationships are toxic to our health and good relationships are nourishing. Now we have science not just confirming that this occurs, but suggesting the actual pathways that support it. Next thing we know, science will convince us we're all One!

Ancient esoteric wisdom has always emphasized the

importance of emotions and the thoughts that accompany our emotions. The Law of Attraction says that our minds are very powerful and what we focus on, with emotion, becomes our reality.

In a nutshell: You are what you think. But how can that be?

What is the Law of Attraction?

The Law of Attraction is one of the Universal Laws that has governed the entire cosmos since the beginning of creation. Although they've called it by different names, many spiritual masters, great artists, musicians, poets, philosophers and others have understood this law and used it in their work or teachings. Today, with the shift that is happening in human consciousness and the knowledge our scientists are gaining about the quantum laws of the physical universe, this metaphysical secret is beginning to become available to the rest of us.

Science and metaphysics agree that vibration is the core, the elemental essence, of everything. The Law of Attraction is about vibration. So what *is* vibration, and what makes it so fundamentally powerful?

You can think of vibration as the pattern that waves make as they radiate from a source. Picture a rock dropped into a pool of water. That's easy to visualize. Now take it a step further and imagine the sound wave created when a drumstick touches a cymbal. In fact, all energy possesses a unique vibrational signature. And for over a century scientists have known that all matter, too, is formed of energy vibrating at specific frequencies.

The powerful fact is these vibrational frequencies don't sit in space in isolation. The Law of Attraction means like attracts like: packets of energy vibrating at a particular frequency attract other packets of energy vibrating at the same frequency.

You are a living magnet. The Law of Attraction says the energy of your thoughts attracts the energy of other thoughts that are similar. In fact, every one of your thoughts, emotions and actions has its own specific vibrational frequency. And each thought, emotion and action resonates with whatever has the same vibrational frequency. Everything that comes to you, you are attracting whether it's something you want or not. You attract people, situations and circumstances that resonate with your vibrational frequency.

Everything that is now solid matter began as a thought, and every day we think approximately sixty thousand thoughts. The fleeting, random thoughts have little effect on us, but the ones we repeat to ourselves over and over and over – the ones we invest with emotion, be it love or fear – have a powerful effect on our health, well-being and motivation. They determine what comes to us.

With practice, you can use the Law of Attraction to manifest anything you desire. You can have, do and be whatever you choose. You can tune yourself to a particular vibrational frequency in order to attract the people, situations and circumstances that will help manifest your desires.

Does that mean mastering some esoteric system of emitting or interpreting vibrational frequencies? Not at all. You don't have to analyze, understand or buy in to a philosophy in order to reap the benefits. The Law of Attraction works whether you believe in it or not. The law of gravity always worked, even before Newton sat under the apple tree and figured it out. Likewise, the Law of Attraction is constantly working. Keep in mind, though: it doesn't judge whether something is good or bad for you. It just delivers whatever you focus on.

The Law of Attraction is an extremely powerful law and it works for every single thing in your life. It applies to everyone and everything. For the purposes of this book, I will focus on the Law of Attraction only as it relates to aging. **I want you to learn to program your mind to harmonize with the Law of Attraction and bring about a younger you.**

What's the catch?

There's only one thing standing in the way: you are already vibrating to a specific frequency, created through many years of programming and conditioning based on your habitual thoughts, feelings and actions. You can't just say "Abracadabra" and change this core vibration. It has shaped you into who you are today, the life circumstances you find yourself in, how you respond to whatever happens to you and how you feel about yourself. This core vibration resonates with whatever you have been programmed to think about growing old; it resonates with whatever your subconscious beliefs are about aging.

The exciting thing is that you *can* take control of the process. And once you take the first steps, you will find – as I have – that you are drawing in support from all corners. The Law of Attraction connects all minds to the Universal Mind, so we have a powerful ally. Spirit, or God, Higher Power, the Universe – whatever name you call that small still voice inside you, will come to your aid in ways you could not possibly have imagined.

In this book you will learn how your thoughts create your reality, how to avoid mental and physical decline, and how to apply the specifics of the Law of Attraction to growing younger. I am intimately aware of the effects fearful and anxious thoughts had on my own health and how the tremendous power of awareness helped turn my life around. When you become conscious of your thoughts, you too can change an aging mindset to a youthful outlook on life and experience the benefits gained by practicing *The Secret Method for Growing Younger*.

EVOLUTION
OF
THIS
PROGRAM

"The materials that surround us in our daily lives mirror the quality of choices that we have made in our lives. Without exception our homes, our automobiles, our pets, and our earth mirror to us, in each moment, the quality, implications and consequences of our life choices."

Gregg Braden, *The Isaiah Effect*

I had been using the Law of Attraction for many years before I began to get inklings for this book. Through my mind and spirit training, I had used the techniques of observing my thoughts and affirming the positive things in my life. Abundance, good relationships, career success, even my physical health responded to the attention I paid to reprogramming my expectations to align with positive energy through the Law of Attraction. **But it never occurred to me to use this Universal**

Law to grow younger.

The image of my mother wasting away with Alzheimer's made a powerful impression on my mind. So did all the other images I had of growing older. Without knowing it, I expected a future of losses and fears, diminishment of all kinds. I accepted it as fact that decline was inevitable, and because of my family's experience with Alzheimer's, somewhere in the back of my mind I rather expected it would happen to me also. I wasn't going to go quietly into the night, though – I would do all I could to keep my body healthy as long as possible, especially by eating right and taking good care of my skin . . . when it was convenient. I knew that exercise was also very important, but, try as I might, I couldn't manage to make it a priority in my life.

And then something happened. A number of years ago I began to notice that my mind seemed to be slipping. It was nothing drastic, but my memory of recent events was less accurate than it had been and I noticed that finding the right words to express myself was becoming troublesome. It worried me enough to go to the doctor and ask for a test.

Some test! He asked me who was President of the United States and what year it was and several other simple and obvious questions. I aced them all and he sent me on my way. I thought the matter was settled until a year later when I applied for long term care insurance. My medical records showed my request for the test and the insurance company wouldn't consider my application unless I submitted to a thorough check of my mind. They sent a nurse to my house and I spent an afternoon being grilled. Sure, I passed. According to medical authorities, I had normal brain functioning for a woman my age.

Still, I *knew* something was different. My clarity of thought was less acute than I was accustomed to. Maybe I shouldn't care, I thought. After all, that's natural, isn't it?

And maybe it was to be expected that, as I got older, I found myself occasionally thinking about what I wouldn't be able to do or be or have when I got up in years. I recall one time in particular when I was considering buying a house near the historic plaza in Taos, New Mexico. I mentioned to two of my daughters that the house would be perfect for me when I got older because it was near the hospital, there were no stairs to climb and it could easily be made wheelchair accessible if we replaced the tub with a walk-in shower.

And then it hit me. What a future I was creating for myself! Because I expected it, I was drawing to myself a reality that meant diminished faculties, reduced mobility and impaired health.

Was that "natural"?

Tapping into Youthful Thoughts

One day a few years ago I was cleaning out the garage

and came across my modeling portfolio. I sat down on a pile of old newspapers and couldn't resist unzipping the portfolio and looking at the fresh unlined face and smooth shoulders of long, long ago. Even though my modeling career was short and took place between the births of my first child and second, I was featured in ads in *Fortune* magazine, *Marie Claire*, *Elle* and *Paris-Match*. It hit home that I would never again look like that young woman in the glossy photographs and I sat there for a while, letting the grief of that realization wash over me.

And then I thought to myself: *Well, Ellen, you have a choice. You can lament your lost youth and live on old memories of what used to be – or you can find a different way to approach getting older. Gracefully easing into old age? That might be wonderful for some people, but not for you. You've always done things differently. You might as well find a different way to handle aging.*

That day in the garage I determined to find different ways to not just slow the aging process, but to truly grow younger. I knew it had nothing to do with the way I looked. However, it had a lot to do with the way I *looked at* how I looked and what my thoughts about myself were.

I knew I had to start from the inside out. *The real fountain of youth is inside me*, I said out loud to no one in that dusty, dirty garage. But I really believe Spirit was listening.

I asked myself: *What if I changed my way of thinking about aging? What if I applied the lessons I had learned from all the teachings and seminars and books and practices to this whole question of aging? What if I applied the Law of Attraction to aging?*

I did, and it worked! The more I practiced, the younger I felt and the more I was capable of. I became deeply intrigued by this whole question of how to reverse aging – how to make the rest of my life even better than the first part. I continued reading and studying to see what other people through the ages had tried – people like the Tibetans, who are rumored to live to a great age with all their faculties intact, and the Okinawans who live and work well into their nineties and beyond.

The practices that made sense to me were the ones I investigated and tried. Slowly, I began to feel like a magnet for ideas and techniques for growing younger. Some showed up in books I read or DVDs I watched; some I heard about through family and friends, but most came as creative insights during my meditations. I began writing the ideas down and practicing them daily.

Those techniques – twenty-one easy-to-practice skills that literally reverse the aging process – will be covered in detail in the new book I am currently writing. They are the branches of a comprehensive program that will help anyone who wants to grow younger.

But the root of the program, the basis upon which your success lies, is offered here. **To truly grow younger, you must reprogram your mind to replace previously-received notions**

of aging with thoughts of the vibrant, joyful, active person you wish to become.   By following the steps in the chapters that follow, you can achieve that and more. You can learn to align your thoughts and actions with a Universal Law and, with the power of the universe behind you, nothing can stop you from your goals.

Remember: You are what you think. If you *worry* about having vitality, stamina, flexibility and strength as you age, you could be praying for what you don't want. If you say, *"Another senior moment,"* when something slips your mind, you might be reinforcing memory decline, and if you *hate* the wrinkles you see in the mirror, that could make you age faster. Abraham, in *Ask and It Is Given: Learning to Manifest Your Desires* by Esther and Jerry Hicks, says it best: "Worrying is using your imagination to get what you don't want."

This book will teach you how to use your imagination to get what you *do* want.

The Steps to Growing Younger

For *Awareness* magazine, Meryl Ann Butler interviewed Dr. Bruce Lipton, a biochemist and a leader in the field of conscious awareness. "While your conscious mind perceives that you are a good driver, it is the unconscious mind that has its hands on the wheel most of the time," observed Dr. Lipton,

"And the unconscious mind may be driving you down the road to ruin."

How do you take control of the aging process and bring your thoughts and actions into alignment with the results you want? The first step is to become aware of the programming that's present in your *conscious* mind. We'll look at that in the next chapter, as you examine your perceptions about aging and explore your fears about the losses and changes it might bring. We'll also take a brief look at the assumptions we, as a society, have of older people.

But, as Dr. Lipton's quote reveals, the bulk of the change has to occur in the subconscious programming. For that, I've developed The 30-Second Grow Younger Method™. This easy-to-use, dependable method is step two in the process. It gives you a way to help recognize how your expectations about aging translate into subconscious programming and it will teach you to gain control of that process by short-circuiting negative programming *as it arises* and consciously reorienting yourself toward the goal of a younger you.

The third step is a *deliberate reprogramming* of your expectations about who you will become with age. This part of the process happens on a deeper level of your subconscious mind. You'll be aided in this step by the Youthfulness Collage and the Creation Planner™. During this creative visualization process, you will allow who you are and who you want to be to unfold. As you progress and find yourself with increased energy and vitality and a clearer mind, that taste of success will give you encouragement to improve other areas, such as your creativity and, yes, even your looks.

These three steps are the essence of *The Secret Method for Growing Younger.* In the final two chapters you'll find some suggestions for habits of mind to help keep you on track, along with recommendations for taking action to help bring about a younger you, and questions to ponder about the potential benefits to humanity when a critical mass of older-generation people pioneers the new frontier of transformation and renewal.

Throughout, I'll weave stories of my experiences with the Law of Attraction to provide encouragement and help you to realize that if I've been able to do this, so can you. Most of all, I want to show you that this is not a solemn, burdensome endeavor. The best way to know if it's working for you is to ask yourself: Am I having fun? Do I feel joyful? If the answer is yes, you're on the right track. There's no better gauge that you *are* growing younger.

EXAMINING YOUR PERCEPTIONS OF OLD AGE

"There are six times as many centenarians per 100,000 people in Okinawa than in the U.S. Okinawans practice a unique blend of Taoism and Confucianism, with women as the acknowledged spiritual leaders. Dr. Bradley Willcox, Harvard physician and researcher, calls theirs a 'practical spirituality' in which the everyday and the divine are closely linked. 'Everything is spiritual – trees, rocks, anything – so that with everything you do, you're connecting with the spirits. They believe in sharing as a society. It's called yuimaru – looking out for one's neighbor – and it's a central theme in the Okinawan value system.' "

"Living Long and Prospering"
Ulysses Torassa, *San Francisco Chronicle*

Who you expect to become as the years advance bears a huge responsibility for who you actually do become. Right now we're on the cusp of greatly expanded longevity. If you're a baby boomer, you may have no intention of growing older like your parents did. But it's probable that you have the mindset of your parents, and the same old images in your mind about what's going to happen to you as you age.

Expecting to grow old is a universal concept. How we expect to be as we age may be different depending on our programming. The first thing we need to do is be aware of what's inside our heads about growing older. Awareness of our perceptions of old age is important in the process of changing our perceptions.

What comes to your mind when you think about getting older? Do you think of losses and fears? Were you even aware that you had programmed images of what it means to be elderly?

I'll give you just some of the images I discovered I had in my mind about aging. See which ones resonate with your picture of what you expect people to experience in their later years. Since I'm a little older than those of you who are baby boomers, I've had even more time to soak up the conditioning.

Here's What I Used to Expect

I fully expected as I advanced in years to have memory

loss, with full-blown Alzheimer's not far behind. And as I mentioned in the previous chapter, I was concerned enough to see a doctor about my difficulty with remembering. Along with the loss of memory, I expected to have less independence and self-esteem and I expected my eyesight and hearing to gradually become impaired. Living in the past, rather than experiencing present-moment awareness, was another image I thought would be part of my later years. I spent many days in nursing homes with my mother and both my mothers-in-law. Before they drifted off into another dimension and were unable to communicate with me, their conversations were always focused on the long-ago past. It was torturous to see those formerly vital, beautiful, loving women unable to even remember recent events like my visit the day before. Is it any wonder I expected to lose my energy and vitality, as well as my mental clarity and agility? Do you see why I now play poker as one of my brain exercises in the twenty-one age-reversing techniques I developed, even though it's only for nickels and dimes?

I imagined that the loss of my skin's dewy freshness and elasticity, and the blooming of a plethora of brown spots, would most likely go hand in hand with loss of libido. The media portrayed older persons with stiff, arthritic joints, or with disease and pain, or with loss of bone density, and those images sunk in. My mind also soaked up ads about curves being in the wrong places, and hair that turns gray as we age, but I didn't see any that

heralded the fun we could have with sex when we no longer had
to worry about becoming pregnant!

What fears did I associate with aging? It's funny, but I
never had a fear of death, which many older folks have. Nor did
I have a fear of retirement, because I always knew that when I
stopped working as a consultant I'd find another way to express
myself because I love working. I never reached the point of
being afraid of slipping and tripping and breaking a hip before I
changed my mental conditioning, but is that a concern for you?
Do you ever worry about being abandoned by your spouse for
a younger woman or man? I have always had a blissful time
meditating and enjoying my own company, a rich social life, and
the pleasure of children and grandchildren to keep me from ever
experiencing loneliness, but does loneliness strike a chord with
you?

A Pause for Inquiry

Spend a few minutes really thinking about what you
expect of someone who is in their later years. Go into your mind
and ask yourself the questions that follow, and others you may
think of, about your impressions of what it means for a person
to be old. Some of your answers may surprise you. There may
be an older person or two who strongly influenced you and your
ideas about growing old. Perhaps that person's way of growing

old was inspiring to you, or perhaps made you feel you never want to get to be that age.

- What does that person look like?
- How does that person feel physically?
- How does that person feel emotionally?
- What is that person's energy level?
- What mental capacity does that person have?
- Does that person have strong relationships?
- What is that person's attitude toward life?
- What motivates that person to get up in the morning?

Truthfully answering these questions gives you the opportunity to look at the underlying beliefs you hold about aging. There's no judgment on your responses, just an examination of what you think about aging, and therefore are expecting. Pay close attention to your emotional reactions brought up by this questioning. Do you have a strong aversion to the loss of memory you witnessed in a loved one? Is there a warm spot in your heart when you think of an elder whose attitude always cheered you up? Do you feel inspired by someone you'd like to emulate as you age? Or are you afraid of getting older? It's these emotions that give power to the beliefs you harbor, creating the expectations that shape your reality.

What Causes Aging?

The root cause of the deterioration and infirmities of growing old is *expecting to be old*. But let's look at some of the ways that translate into specific aging effects.

We all know that mental stress is detrimental to our health and appearance. Our bodies possess a perfect mechanism for dealing with stress that saves us from a physical attack. If we are frightened by a potential attack, our fight-or-flight mechanism kicks in. Our bodies produce a higher level of cortisol, which in turn causes our blood pressure and blood sugar to rise, providing the energy we need to escape that crocodile nipping at our toes. The physical energy expended uses up the extra cortisol and our hormone levels return to normal. But what if the stress is strictly mental? We still produce just as much cortisol, but with no physical activity to use up its by-products, we are stuck with elevated blood pressure, elevated blood sugar and a suppressed immune system. An obsession with the fear of aging and death can also contribute to mental stress, as do selfishness, mishandling anger, holding grudges and entertaining negative thoughts. All these factors can lead to rapid aging.

The physical stresses of gravity and loss of skin collagen and elasticity are compounded by insufficient and/or poor quality sleep, too much sun, lack of exercise, poor diet and not drinking enough water.

And here's a real aging biggie: not having enough fun! Not laughing enough! Having fun is the one thing I've been able to *really* master to help me grow younger. Fun is my middle name.

For all of these causes there are solutions to help you reverse the effects of aging. Some of the solutions available to you are extreme biological manipulations that cost many thousands of dollars each year. There are a number of books available that will give you information on those solutions, but those are not the solutions that form the basis for this book or my next.

Aging Differently

Most of us just allow aging to happen. We don't even consciously think about it – except when we look in the mirror and tell ourselves we don't like what we see. But our subconscious minds are aware of what we think and feel about aging. Our subconscious minds are packed full of images and ideas and expectations for growing older, as you've discovered in the exercise provided earlier in this chapter.

We got most of those ideas from our parents and grandparents, but we don't need to keep those images. We can be different! Think about the ways that you are different from your parents. Did your father serve in the armed forces – and did you march against the war in the 1960s? Were your parents

God-fearing folks – while you became intimate with a loving God who lives inside of you? Did you love rock and roll (and still do), but your parents couldn't stand that noise?

Well, perhaps you're meant to age differently from your parents, too.

From the day I was born, I was always different. I was different from what my mother was hoping and praying for during the long nine months before delivery. The story was told to me many times about the day I was born at home in 1936. The doctor was there and so was my father. As soon as I was born, my father quickly covered my bottom to give my mother a few more moments before finding out it's a girl! (moan, groan). Then my father said, in his broken English accent, "I no care if it is a girl, she's a little doll."

His comment was always included when the story was told so I wouldn't feel too bad about disappointing my mother.

My being different began that day. I was different from what my parents expected of me. My mother, perhaps like your mother, didn't have a career. And because I was a girl, and my parents were old-country, they expected that I would finish high school, get a job as a secretary, get married and raise children, and live near my folks.

Instead, my high school counselor lined up scholarships to college for me and I fully expected to attend Syracuse University to become a journalist. And then it happened! I got pregnant.

It was my senior year in high school and although the baby lived only two days, it dashed all hopes for college. In those days you weren't even allowed to attend high school if you were pregnant, but I managed to attend all but the last month. Even so, all college scholarships were embarrassingly withdrawn.

Old-country folks, from Czechoslovakia. Their good name was extremely important, and I brought a great shame to the family. But – and this is the surprising part – they never, ever condemned me for it. They were kind and loving and gentle toward me. My father did a lot more sighing and oy-yoy-yoying than normal and it seemed his hair turned white overnight, but both my mother and father treated me tenderly and the kids in my senior class behaved toward me with kindness and respect.

The following fall my mother went to work in the five and dime so I could attend business school. Although I was trained to be a secretary, I began my career as a copywriter, because I had started a student newspaper at the business school and the woman who owned the business school had a brother who owned the radio station and *voilà*!

A short time later, I moved to New York City, married and had four children as was expected of me, but my being different also extended to starting a business at home in New Jersey with my husband when my baby was still an infant. We made sculpture puzzles and games in our barn and I did all the selling, marketing and bookkeeping. Society frowned on women who worked in those days, especially if the kids stayed at home while mother went to work. The selling part of my job took me out of the house – sometimes with the children and sometimes without.

If it was after school hours, we'd pack up the kids in the Volkswagen bus and my husband would drive me from gift shop to gift shop and they'd wait in the bus while I went into the shop to sell. But if I had a meeting with a buyer at Bloomingdale's or Saks Fifth Avenue in New York, the kids stayed at home with my husband or a good friend. The women's movement hadn't yet taken hold and my leaving the children at home to go out and sell was against society's rules, but I loved working.

Even if you've never once questioned the way things "ought to be", there's no time like the present to start. When it comes to growing younger, you've got nothing to lose – and everything to gain.

Vive La Difference!

Today I celebrate being different. Taking risks, doing the unexpected, is good for the brain and helps you grow younger. I continue to stand out from the crowd with my passion for the metaphysical. All that excited talk about *everything happening simultaneously* and about *thoughts being things* has brought me my fair share of eye-rolling and little "woo woo" sounds from friends and colleagues whose experience has led them to different destinations. But their teasing is good-natured, and I take those gestures and sounds as signs of affection.

It is important to startle your brain! Thrill to the excitement of being different. Laugh at fear. Take risks. It makes you feel alive! Make new grooves in your brain by eating with your left hand, if you normally eat with your right. Dye your hair a different color. Take up painting or drama or sign up for a class that no one would ever expect you to take, like belly dancing or wind surfing. Start a poker game in your neighborhood. Science has proven that the combination of mental strategy and socializing in a poker game is excellent for growing younger. Do it for nickels, dimes and quarters as my group does, and *expect* to win – but if occasionally you don't, you won't lose the grocery money playing for small change.

If there is something that you love doing, you just have to jump off the deep end and do it. I had to remind myself of that last weekend. I was getting ready to go to the Oscar party in Taos with my friend Mike. It was a swanky affair, the newspaper said, *so get out your fancy duds and win a prize for best dressed.* I was planning to wear my body-forming silver-sequined gown with a side slit so deep a woman half my age would think twice about wearing it, and a matching art deco-style silver headdress with hanging beaded fringe. I love that outfit. I bought it in 1982 and I feel so glamorous in it, plus I don't have to fix my hair; the headdress covers it.

As I was getting dressed, the old programming, old conditioning, flashed into my mind and I wondered about the appropriateness of a seventy-year-old woman wearing an outfit like that. And just as quickly, my new thinking about aging took over and assured me it didn't matter. This was to be a fun event and that outfit was fun to wear. Besides, I had the perfect coat to wear with it: my full-length white "mink" that I got on sale from a catalog for $94 (it's even machine washable!) So I put on the silver outfit and the coat, Mike and I went to the Oscar party, and we won best dressed couple!

Old programming continues to rear its head from time to time for me, just as it did on Oscar night. But it happens far less frequently than it used to. And for you? In this chapter you've looked at the conditioning that you feel may be lodged in your subconscious. Now it's time to start practicing the steps in the chapters that follow so **you can become that vibrant, sexy, capable older person you know you can be.**

CHANGING FOCUS:
THE 30-SECOND
GROW YOUNGER
METHOD™

"There is no condition so severe that you cannot reverse it by choosing different thoughts. However, choosing different thoughts requires focus and practice. If you continue to focus as you have been, to think as you have been, and to believe as you have been, then nothing in your experience will change."

Esther and Jerry Hicks

Ask and It Is Given: Learning to Manifest Your Desires

You should pause a minute and give yourself credit. It's hard work, pulling to the surface those deeply rooted thoughts and fears about aging. By facing them, fully acknowledging their existence, and then gently questioning their validity, you've taken the first major step toward growing younger. You've taken a long hard look at the powerlessness almost all of us associate with aging. **Now it's time to claim the power of growing younger.**

The trouble is, those impressions and images you have accumulated in your mind over the years have worn grooves in your brain and are magnetically attracting those negative characteristics to you. If you expect that your skin will begin to lose elasticity and your energy level will begin to diminish, that is what is being drawn to you. If you expect the number and depth of your wrinkles to increase and the aches and pains in your joints to multiply, that is what is on its way to you. If you have noticed your memory slipping and have anxiety about Alzheimer's or other forms of dementia, that is what you have to look forward to in your future, **unless you change your focus every time you have one of those thoughts.** You must continue doing it until a younger you becomes second nature in your mind.

Thirty Seconds to a Younger You

In this chapter you will learn to observe your thoughts and recognize when you are reinforcing the images you do not want. You will also make new grooves in your brain and new magnetic pathways to your subconscious mind. The Law of Attraction is *always* doing its job, without judgment, without regard to outcomes. It always magnetically attracts what you focus on, and if you change your focus, it will change what it brings you to match your new focus.

True, it's not quite as easy as that. You have spent years with those thoughts and beliefs, so it will take diligence and continual training to change your belief system. To grow younger, you need to become aware of your current automatic thoughts about aging *each time they occur* and then reprogram your mind with thoughts you choose to have. The way to do this is explained in the following step-by-step process I developed called The 30-Second Grow Younger Method™. I adapted it from the approach I used to develop an abundance mentality and, although I have been using the Grow Younger Method for only a few years, through repetition I have trained my mind to be alert to any thoughts or words that might undermine my desire to grow younger.

And I am younger! I have much more energy, vitality and flexibility than I had even thirty years ago. If I choose to, I can work as many hours as I did when I was thirty-five without feeling fatigue. My mind is clearer and sharper than it was and I'm flexible enough to handle any changes in life that come my way. Not only that, I can dance as exuberantly as I did when I was thirty-five. (Just ask my dog, Colitta – she watches me every night when I turn on the stereo and dance to disco while I make dinner.)

Oh, I can hear you asking me: But do you *look* thirty-five? Right now, I'll tell you honestly, I do not. I've often been told I look younger than my years, but thirty-five? Not even close. Do I think it's *possible* to look thirty-five or twenty-five? Yes, I do, because the Law of Attraction never fails. Although I am practicing age-reversing techniques to give my body, mind and spirit the advantages of youthfulness, I don't know how long it will take to overcome my powerful mental conditioning that says looking thirty-five when I'm seventy is probably impossible. I'll say this much – if the universe wants to make me look thirty-five or even twenty-five, that's fine with me! And if my face and body do *not* take on the appearance of a thirty-five-year-old, that's fine with me, too. I love who I am right now and I am very grateful for *all* of my life. But I will continue practicing The 30-Second Grow Younger Method™. It has worked miracles for me so far and I expect it to continue doing so.

The five steps of The 30-Second Grow Younger Method™ can be accomplished in as little as thirty seconds. You can practice this method anywhere, whether you're at home, on the train, stuck in rush-hour traffic, in the movie theater, on the beach – anywhere. You can practice it whether you are alone or with someone. Thirty seconds is a short time, so even if you're with someone who is not like-minded and who may not understand, you can still take thirty seconds without their knowing what you're up to.

If you are with someone who has an open heart and open mind, *do* tell that person what you are doing. It is an important part of manifestation to tell other people your expectation. That will add the force and energy of their emotions and thoughts to your expectation, even if they are hesitant to believe you at first.

A brief synopsis of the 30-Second Grow Younger Method is provided in the box below as a convenient one-page reference. Details of each of the steps follow.

THE 30-SECOND
GROW YOUNGER METHOD™

1. Catch yourself.

Notice a thought that you look old, feel old or have a memory lapse – or that you will in the future.

2. Center your awareness in the middle of your forehead.

Let go of the negative thought – without judgment - and allow your consciousness to drift to your forehead.

3. Say: "With every breath I take, the cells in my body grow younger."

Say it out loud or silently.

4. Feel the emotion of a younger you.

Straighten your posture. Re-live a positive feeling you had when you were in your prime.

5. Say: "Thank you. Thank you. Thank you."

Feel your gratitude as you say it.

Putting the Steps into Practice

Use The 30-Second Grow Younger Method™ any time you have a thought or say something that reinforces the old programming for aging. It may be quite frequent at first and the words may actually breeze past your lips, but with continual practice of the five steps, those thoughts and words will become less and less frequent. Soon you'll notice when others say something that strengthens the old way of aging and you'll silently say to yourself: cancel, cancel.

Let's go through each step, one by one.

1. Catch yourself.

Before you can reprogram your mind, you need to make yourself consciously aware when you are thinking, saying, feeling or doing anything that reinforces a negative mindset about getting older. Catching yourself means noticing. Notice your thoughts, notice your emotions, notice your words. Notice your actions and your reactions. The art of noticing must be cultivated and practiced. Continual noticing will increase your awareness, which means bringing your thoughts, words, emotions, actions and reactions to a conscious level. When you bring everything to a conscious level, you are **expanding your consciousness.** This is where you want to live, day in and day out, because here, in this state of expanded consciousness and expanded awareness, is where we have choices about the reality we want to live in. From here you can choose.

You need to make it a habit to catch yourself. For example, when you look in the mirror, notice when you are telling yourself you don't like the way you look. *Oh dear, look at that – I have another wrinkle.* You might have sex problems and think: *Oh dear, I guess it's to be expected. I'm getting old. Oh dear, I don't have the energy I used to have. Oh dear, another senior moment. Oh dear, I hope I don't get Alzheimer's like my mother did. Oh dear, oh dear, oh dear.*

Stop it. If you can just get into the habit of doing that – interrupting your thoughts from telling you negative things about yourself – that's a huge start. You cannot reprogram your mind unless you interrupt the thoughts, words and emotions you don't want, then deprogram your mind.

Every time you verbalize or think thoughts that express an image you don't want about growing old, catch yourself. Make yourself aware of those words or thoughts. Don't criticize yourself and don't judge. Self-recrimination uses up good energy. Just *be aware*.

2. Center your awareness in the middle of your forehead.

Release it. Let go of the negative thought or emotion. Or interrupt the words – in mid-sentence, if necessary. Let your focus drift to the center of your forehead. You may feel a sensation between your brows or you may feel nothing. Don't expect anything, don't force any feeling, just allow your consciousness to dwell there for a moment. Allow yourself to just *be*. As the chatter of your mind begins to still and the sensations of your body fade away, you'll begin to really be in the here and now. In fact, nowhere else exists. The past is gone; the future is not yet here. All you have is this present moment.

3. Say: "*With every breath I take, the cells in my body grow younger.*"

Words are powerful. Say these words out loud if you're alone, because there is magic and power in sound. Or you can say them silently – with the intention that they will have all the magic and power of spoken words.

If you have words you feel are more powerful than these for growing younger, say them. The exact words I was inspired to use are, "*With every breath I take, the cells in my body vibrate at a high rate and grow younger,*" and I feel they are working for me. If you have a scientific background, my affirmation may not be right for you because you know that every day 300 billion cells in our bodies die and new ones emerge, and your mind may not be able to wrap around having *all* your cells grow younger at the same time. Then instead of getting the benefit from the affirmation, you'll get stuck trying to figure out: *How in the world can I have 300 billion cells die today and yet they're all growing younger? And vibrating. At a higher rate. Hmm. That doesn't make any sense. If some are wearing out and dying, and some are just being born . . .* And the next thing you know, your mind is off chewing on chatter, instead of peacefully affirming youthfulness.

Keep in mind that, when reprogramming your mind, it may not work to say, *I am 25 years old. I have the face and body of a twenty-five-year-old.* Your mind might not believe you. You need to start out with small affirmations such as: *I know the cells in my body are growing younger. I can't see them, but just as I know that the vitamins I took are affecting my body in a positive way, I know that my thoughts are helping me grow younger.*

And it's okay to look in the mirror and say: *You're gorgeous, you sexy babe!* Or, *My, you're a handsome fellow!*

If you can truly love who you are and how you look right now, then youthfulness will come to you far more quickly. In fact, it is critically important to love how you look right now. You might have wrinkles, age spots, or gray hair. Love them! They are part of who you are right now.

Otherwise, if you look in the mirror and don't like what you see, your mind will wrap around all the negative thoughts and feelings you have about aging and block out any positive affirmations toward growing younger and then the Law of Attraction will bring you more of the same – looks you don't like.

Anytime you find yourself criticizing or thinking poorly

of yourself, it helps to remember the story of the elderly Chinese woman and her two large pots. Every day she put a pot on each end of a pole which she carried across her shoulders, and she'd take the long walk to the stream to get water. One of the pots had a crack in it, while the other pot was perfect. At the end of the long walk back, the perfect pot always arrived home with a full portion of water, while the cracked pot was only half full.

This went on daily for two whole years. Each day, the woman arrived home with only one and a half pots of water.

Of course, the perfect pot was very proud of its achievements, but the poor cracked pot was ashamed of its imperfection, and felt quite miserable that it could accomplish only half of what it had been created to do.

One day, after two years of what felt like absolute failure, the cracked pot spoke to the woman. It confessed, "I am so ashamed of myself. I have this ugly thin crack in my side which causes water to leak out all the way home and I always arrive only half full."

The woman smiled. She said to the pot, "Did you notice that there are flowers on your side of the path, but not on the other pot's side? I've always known about your thin crack, so I planted flower seeds on your side of the path, and every day while we walk back, you water them. For two years I've been able to pick these beautiful flowers to decorate the table.

"Because you are perfect just the way you are, we are able

to have this beauty to grace our house."

Remember that loving yourself *as you are* – even if it's an effort and something you can manage only some of the time – is a key part of this method.

Let me tell you a story of a time I forgot this. For about five months, I had been conscientiously practicing Tibetan exercises – part of my age-reversing techniques -- and saying my *Masters of the Far East* affirmations. Every day after my shower I'd look in the mirror, hoping to see some signs of growing younger, but all that would stare back at me were wrinkles and sagging skin.

I was dismayed. Where were the results I was looking for?

And then it hit me! Of course I would not continue to grow younger: my thoughts were on what I looked like, and I didn't like what I saw. I was fretting that my skin was not becoming more youthful, no matter how many exercises I performed or how many affirmations I said. The Law of Attraction worked! It brought me exactly what I focused on: wrinkles and sagging skin.

I had been working with the Law of Attraction for years and I knew what I needed to do. I absolutely believe that I am a field of pure potentiality and I know that literally everything I see around me is a manifestation of my consciousness. I needed to change my focus and open up to allow Spirit's answer to my affirmation requests to manifest.

Disliking my looks and checking for results had to stop. I began concentrating on the pure pleasure of practicing the techniques, staying focused in the here and now, while *feeling* the emotions I had experienced in my prime. I also began to affirm that I am extremely grateful for who I am, what I look like and the joy I have in my heart.

When you practice the techniques in this book, change will begin on the *inside* of you. The Law of Attraction is a creative force from the Universal Mind that flows through each of us at all times. As you continue to expand your consciousness and connect with Spirit on a continual basis, you will also *glow* on the outside with radiant beauty. There is no cream or cosmetic, no treatment that can give a greater glow to your skin, a greater warmth and softness to your eyes, than the realization of love for yourself and connectedness to all life. With that knowledge firmly planted on the inside, the fruits are a smile that warms and words that heal. You will be beautiful, because your thoughts and actions are beautiful and you will be perceived as beautiful by those who behold you and bask in your light. **It's all a reflection of *who you are on the inside.***

4. Feel the emotion of a younger you.

Just briefly, visualize a time when you were in your prime and it made you feel fabulous. You will be able to do this quickly and easily after you have set up your Youthfulness Collage and

Creation Planner™ as shown in the following chapter. For the fourth step in The 30-Second Grow Younger Method™, you just want to *feel* the emotion. This is not the time for extensive creative visualization; that will happen during a longer period once a day. What you want now is to reconnect with the emotion. Straighten your posture and let the emotion of a younger you zip up and down your body.

It is vitally important that you bring all of yourself to the fore. The more you can really re-experience the feeling, remembering the sights, sounds, smells, gazes of those around you, the tingling in your stomach, the joy in your heart, the energy in your younger body, the sparkle in your eyes, the more easily you will lodge this feeling. It needs to "take," to land in you just as if it were happening for the very first time, *at this very moment.* Your emotions are a powerful "creativity catalyst" and it is very important that you are aware of applying that force. If it is appropriate, close your eyes to experience this emotion.

The memory I use is from a time when I lived in New York City in 1960. I was modeling then and on one particular day I was walking along Fifth Avenue on my way to the model agency. I remember I had on a red hat – a beret that was perched on the side of my head. A pickup truck drove by and a guy sitting in the back shouted, "Hi, Frenchie!" That's all he said and the truck continued on its way. It wasn't just him or his remark that lodged in my brain. That day I felt on top of the world, new, fresh, joyful and happy to be alive. What makes that day different from today is that I also had a youthful appearance, so I use that particular instance to feel the emotion of a younger me. I see the Fifth Avenue store windows, the people on the crowded sidewalks. I see myself dressed smartly with a red suit and my little red beret. I smell the Manhattan smells, perfume wafting from a passerby, chestnuts roasting on the street vendor's wagon. I hear the traffic and the particular sounds that are peculiarly New York, and I hear "Hi, Frenchie!" as I see his truck pass by. By engaging all my senses, the emotion of that day becomes embedded in my subconscious and helps the Law of Attraction do its job of bringing about a younger me.

Search your memory and find your own particular day when you felt fresh and new and young. Go through a photo album if that is helpful. Then use all your senses to *feel* the emotion of a younger you. Remember, you are building up a field of energy. Energy follows intention, and when you focus your intention on a younger you, you sow the field for the creation of youthfulness. As this field strengthens, its magnetic power grows and grows. This, then, acts as an attractor for youthfulness.

5. Say: "Thank you. Thank you. Thank you."

Express your gratitude with these words, silently or out loud, and combine it with a deep reverence and a loving attitude. By saying "Thank you!" you are affirming the fact that you *notice* that you truly are blessed. You are also producing a beautiful, clear vibration with those words.

By expressing appreciation, your mind affects your physical body and sends healing to all the cells in your body. Studies on gratitude are being done at The HeartMath Institute, a global leader in researching the critical link among emotions, heart-brain communication and cognitive function. Their research shows that by cultivating the positive emotions of gratitude, you can actually improve your heart's rhythmic functioning.

In his book *The Hidden Messages in Water*, Japanese researcher Dr. Masaru Emoto details the findings of his research showing the effects of human vibrational energy, including thoughts, words, ideas and music, on the molecular structure of water. The resulting photographs of the crystalline structures of water following exposure to particular positive or negative words and thoughts will surely make you a believer in the effects of your words and thoughts on absolutely everything in and around you.

In an interview with Dr. Emoto for *The Spirit of Ma'at*, Reiko Myamoto Dewey asked if he knew of a particular word or phrase that was most beneficial in cleaning up the natural waters in the world. Dr. Emoto replied, "Yes. There is a special combination that seems to be perfect for this, which is *love* plus the combination of thanks and appreciation reflected in the English word *gratitude*. Just one of these is not enough. Love needs to be based in gratitude and gratitude needs to be based in love. These two words together create the most important vibration." Dr. Emoto goes on to say that each spoken word has its own vibration, as does each written word. "Beautiful words have beautiful, clear vibrations. But negative words put out ugly, incoherent vibrations," he says, a finding that is illustrated by the studies shown in his book.

It's been my habit to say "Thank you" throughout the day to seemingly inanimate objects. When I make my smoothie in the morning, I thank each ingredient I add into the blender, from the flax seed to the frozen banana and all six other ingredients in between. Even if it doesn't *really* make the smoothie tastier, it does create a joyous emotion in my body. In addition, I was influenced by Dr. Emoto's book to always say, "I love you, water; thank you, water," when I fill my water bottle several times a day. When I am focusing on telling the water in my bottle that I love it, there is no room in my mind for other, nonproductive, non-fun chatter.

Those five steps complete *The 30-Second Grow Younger Method*™. Perhaps in the beginning it will take a minute or two, but through constant repetition, it will become second nature and take no more than thirty seconds each time. It took me quite some time before I was able to do it in thirty seconds flat, so take heart if mastering this practice doesn't happen right away. And if you find that some days you just keep forgetting to catch yourself, *that's okay*! Laugh it off and try again the next day.

POWERFUL TRANSFORMATION TOOLS: YOUTHFULNESS COLLAGE AND THE CREATION PLANNER™

"One of the most important steps in making your
creative visualization work effectively and successfully
is to have the feeling of being connected with
your inner spiritual source. Your spiritual source
is the supply of infinite love, wisdom, and energy
in the universe. For you, *source* may mean God,
Goddess, universal intelligence, the Great Spirit, the
higher power, or your true essence. However we
conceptualize it, it can be found here and now within
each of us, in our inner beings."

Shakti Gawain, *Creative Visualization*

In the previous chapter you learned how to use The
30-Second Grow Younger Method™ to consciously interrupt
negative programming *when the thought occurs* and consciously

change your thoughts so you can attract the vibrational frequency that will help bring about youthfulness. In my practice of this method, I have to keep reminding myself that growing younger is a process, not an event, and that I need to develop this change in consciousness gradually.

If you've ever driven a car with a manual shift, you know you can't have the gear shift in first and then go directly into fourth gear. You'll stall the car (I learned that when I was sixteen), and the car won't move forward. You need to start in first gear, then go smoothly into second, then into third and finally into fourth. Once in a while, you can go from first to third and the car responds beautifully, just as a few of you will be able to make a quantum leap and touch that inner source, that place inside where magic happens, and immediately create a fresh, younger you. But for the rest of us, it's best to shift one gear at a time, whether it's your car or your consciousness.

We need not only to shift gradually, we also need to use all the tools we possibly can to bring about this transformation, because our minds are so accustomed to growing older, rather than growing younger. No doubt at times you've heard someone say, "Someday I'm going to live in a beautiful mansion like that one." Or, "Even though I have a heart problem, I'm going to beat it and one of these days I'll be in perfect health." Or, "I am going to be rich!" Or "Someday I'm going to have a fancy car like that." Or, "I *know* there's a man out there for me." Or, "I don't have a penny to my name right now, but I can see myself vacationing in the south of France and fly-fishing off my 40-foot yacht."

And so, people who were poor *have* been able to become rich, own beautiful mansions, have fancy cars and yachts and vacation in the south of France. And people who were ill, or even dying, have been able to bring themselves to perfect health. And single men and women who seemed destined to remain forever single have found mates.

But have you ever heard someone say, "Someday I'm going to be young!" Or, "My mind is becoming clearer and sharper as I age." Or, "Every birthday my body seems to get stronger and more flexible." Or, "My energy level keeps increasing year after year." Or, from someone who is over fifty, "Sex gets better the older I get."

Not likely! Nor did I think to question how I was programming my mind around Alzheimer's or expecting to have a diminished life in my later years, even though I had been studying and applying the Law of Attraction most of my adult life.

I *know* that the Law of Attraction works all the time, but it can take some time to get used to this realization. We need to allow this to gradually seep into our consciousness, and not be bowled over by it so that we reject it without giving it a fair opportunity to work for us and help us grow younger. According to the workings of the Law of Attraction, everything you see is the result of the Law of Attraction at work. All your thoughts have materialized into who you are and the circumstances in which you find yourself. In the lesson I am studying today in *A Course in Miracles*, it says, "Everything you see is the result of your thoughts. There is no exception to this fact." Since we're told the Law of Attraction never fails, and I truly believe that, there is no reason why we cannot use it to grow younger.

Granted, it may be more difficult than a poor man becoming rich, or a terminally ill woman recovering totally, or a childless couple having a baby, because our minds can conceive of those things happening. What this book is proposing we do is change what our minds can conceive, and expect to manifest what has hitherto been considered impossible. Right now we live in the age of the impossible becoming possible. We live in the age of miracles.

I, too, thought it was impossible to grow younger, but I don't think that any longer. I *know* it's possible because it is working for me. However, I am not finished deliberately working with the Law of Attraction to create youthfulness, since I want to touch that inner source, that fountain of youth, and become brand new. Not brand new *again*. Not become a younger version of who I am today, but to merge with my inner source and become a person wholly living in the present moment and enjoying all the fun of being a youthful companion to the universe.

I have been training my mind for a few years now, so thoughts of growing old with diminished capacity and doubts about whether I can grow young are far fewer. Vibrant thoughts of youthfulness are beginning to become more and more automatic. I need to use The 30-Second Grow Younger Method™ much less frequently and, with persistent practice, you will find the same thing happening. It is my joyous desire to have you, and everyone else in the world, benefit not just from being young, but from experiencing the incredible joy that the Law of Attraction brings when we get in touch with that inner source of youthfulness.

Fundamentals for Change

Whenever you have doubts that you will be able to influence the aging process using the power of your mind, be gentle with yourself. I have certainly experienced moments like that. The job is then to acknowledge the doubts and **continue trying**. And because it is a huge shift to go from not believing that growing young is possible to actually becoming young, I strongly recommend you supplement your practice of The 30-Second Grow Younger Method™ with a daily twenty-minute creative visualization process. This creative visualization process will allow you to go deeper and strengthen your connection to the energy that is shifting your vibrational frequency. This energy is your inner spiritual source. For this part of the process you will use the Creation Planner™ and your Youthfulness Collage.

The Creation Planner™ gives you the opportunity to specify exactly what you desire of a younger you, or – if you prefer – open yourself to allow what Spirit wants to bring you. The Creation Planner™ will also help increase your vibrational frequency to match the frequency of youthfulness. One important thing to keep in mind about the Creation Planner™ is that the Universe is the Planner. **You give the order and the Universe will plan exactly how a younger you will come about.** The Universe will plan the "how" and send you promptings and clues for you to take action, which you'll learn about in the next chapter. The Creation Planner™ works only with energy, though. For now, actions are not part of this process.

Creating time in your life that you commit to this process is perhaps the most important step. Twenty minutes a day is not very much time, but you may be surprised to notice how little things can keep cropping up to distract you, if you have not made a clear agreement with yourself to show up. The Creation Planner™ is one of the most powerful processes in this book, so please give it a fair trial. Make a commitment to give yourself this time every day for two weeks, then assess the value you're receiving. There's no hard work involved, just a willingness to keep returning to your commitment.

I find the daily 20-minute part of the growing younger process so valuable that most days I spend half an hour in the morning and half an hour in the evening with the practice. Even though I have a very busy life, the time I spend with this creative visualization technique is incredibly productive, not just for becoming youthful but, for enhancing all of my life.

The first time you use the Creation Planner™ and the Youthfulness Collage, give yourself extra time to set them up and learn the process. This will become a simple streamlined process once you know the steps. You won't need more than twenty minutes once you've made it a regular habit.

Getting Started With Your Youthfulness Collage and Creation Planner™

The Youthfulness Collage and Creation Planner™ are two dynamic tools that you create to help guide the process of growing younger. They can be as simple or as elaborate as you like and each one will be as unique as its creator.

Here are the tools you need to make the Creation Planner™:

- One zippered three-ring binder with an outside pocket
- Clear plastic CD-holder sleeves with pockets and three holes, sized to fit the binder
- One sheet of 1" x 4" labels
- A pen and markers

- One package of 3" x 5" cards

For the Youthfulness Collage you also need:
- Posterboard, cut to 11" x 17", white or a color of your choice
- Glue stick
- Scissors

In addition, you need a clear space to work on your Youthfulness Collage and Creation Planner™ and twenty minutes you can set aside each day for this process. You may purchase these items individually or, if you prefer, you can visit my website at *www.howtogrowyounger.com* to order a complete kit.

Setting Up Your Youthfulness Collage

Step 1.

Score and fold the posterboard in half so that it forms an 8½" x 11" book.

Step 2.

On the front cover, use a marker to write a title that means something to you. If you have a name now, go ahead and write it on the cover. Or you may choose to wait and allow a name to come later. For our purposes, I will call it your Youthfulness Collage.

Step 3.

Open up your book, and look at the inside. It's empty! This is where you get to have fun placing images that represent the new you. Here is an opportunity to create your life in a place that is not limited by ideas and images from the past, so enjoy the freedom of that blank page. Start building a new picture of the life you imagine for yourself.

Step 4.

The next part you may do during one day, or it may take days or weeks to accomplish. You are going to gather images or printed words that represent the feeling that you'd like to have in your life. Notice them. You may be reading a magazine and find a picture of something that inspires you. Cut out that picture and save it for your Youthfulness Collage. Maybe there's a word or phrase you see printed somewhere that evokes a fresh, youthful image; cut that out and save it.

Recognize images that contain clues to the inner you, images that stimulate your own feeling of youthfulness. It can be helpful to have a folder or an envelope that you keep with you throughout the day, so you can easily organize the images you want. Keep in mind that the content of these images doesn't matter as much as the feeling you get from them. If you have photos of yourself when you were younger that evoke a *feeling* of freshness, aliveness and fun, include those as well.

Step 5.

When you're ready to start arranging images, open your Youthfulness Collage and place the images you've collected on the table before you. Have some fun arranging them on the board of your Youthfulness Collage. Perhaps you'll notice that certain combinations of images express unexpected themes; in that case you might use one corner of the board to represent one area of youthfulness, another corner to represent some other aspect.

Most of all, keep it *fun*! Nobody's watching so go ahead and express yourself in the most imaginative way you can. Sure, I felt a little silly at first, and you may too, cutting pictures and words out of magazines and catalogs like a four-year-old. But after awhile I felt the enormous freedom of doing something whimsical and childlike – a far cry from the adult burden of "work" – and it actually made my whole body tingle with the sensation of being young and having fun.

Step 6.

After you have arranged things the way you like, use the glue stick on the back of the images and stick them down on the board. It's okay if images overlap each other — that can be part of the fun. You might start with a picture of a bottle of wine pouring into a glass, and then glue down a glass slipper over the wine goblet. Use your imagination! These are images that mean something to you alone. They don't have to make sense to anyone else.

You might want to consider this dynamic tool a work in progress. Keep on adding words and images at various times, or even start a new one if you find images that have relevance and there's no more room on the collage. Allow it to be a living work of art. The growth and change it makes over time can give you as much pleasure as the initial set up.

Now that you've created your Youthfulness Collage, or at least have a good start on it, what do you do with it? As you'll learn in the next section, it is an important part of the Creation Planning Exercises. In addition, you may want to look at it throughout the day by placing it where it's easily seen, unless it contains images that are very private to you. If it does, that's good! It is important to explore feelings that you may not have even allowed *yourself* permission to feel, much less let other people know about. The images in your collage are not an advertisement to tell the world what you want; it is the magic mirror that tells you that you – yes, *you* – are the most beautiful or handsome person in the world, with all the vitality, stamina, flexibility, energy and sexiness of a person in their prime. If your collage *is* private, at the end of your Creation Planning Exercises each day, fold it up and place it inside the Creation Planner™.

Setting Up Your Creation Planner™

Step 1.

Gather together the parts of your Creation Planner™ on a table where there are no other items to distract you. I prefer to make a delightful ritual of this process and the exercises that follow and you may want to also. In my meditation room where I do these exercises, I have a special altar chock full of items that have special significance for me. My altar is very eclectic with photos of my kids, my parents, Jesus, Mary and Joseph, St. Germaine, the Dalai Lama, the Karmapa and Yongey Mingyur Rinpoche; statues of Buddha, Green Tara, Quan Yin, Merlin and several frogs; a clay dragon and other clay creatures made by two of my grandchildren; crystals and stones of all kinds including a piece of the Himalayas and a plain, old American rock given to me by someone special; candles and incense. You don't have to go crazy with this (as you might think I have) but do whatever works for you.

Step 2.

The clear plastic sleeves should have CD-holder pockets, which will be used for holding the 3" x 5" cards. On one of the 1" x 4" labels, write "Affirmations," and affix it to the top of a clear plastic sleeve. On another label, write "Creations", and attach it to another plastic sleeve.

Step 3.

Next you will write some affirmations. Affirmations are words or phrases you repeat that have deep meaning for you. You hold them in your conscious mind, but repetition allows them to sink into your subconscious. Affirmations that begin with "I am" are very powerful commands to the Universe.

Write your favorite affirmations on 3" x 5" cards – one per card. You will add new affirmations as you progress, so do not be too concerned about which affirmations you use in the beginning. Keep all current ones in the sleeve labeled "Affirmations."

Here are some affirmation suggestions to get you started. You may also go to my website www.howtogrowyounger.com and click on Affirmations for even more.

- With every breath I take, the cells in my body grow younger.

- I magnetize people, situations and circumstances that support my desire to be young.

- I recognize, understand and follow Spirit's guidance.

- I am Love, Joy, Youth and Radiant Beauty.

- I am Perfect Health, Sensuality and Spirituality.

- I am Wit and Wisdom.

- Infinite Joy fills my mind and *thrills* my body with its perfect life. From *Life and Teaching of the Masters of the Far East*, vol. 1, Baird T. Spaulding.

Please share your favorites with our online community!

Enjoy the Journey

Now that your Youthfulness Collage and Creation Planner™ are ready to use, it's time to get started doing the exercises. These are part of the creative visualization process that works with your subconscious mind on a deep level to reinforce youthfulness and help you discover *who you really are*.

Here is a summary of the Creation Planning Exercises. The details of each step follow; however, I wanted you to have an overview on one page that is easy to refer to.

CREATION PLANNING EXERCISES

1. Get comfortable. Open your collage in front of you. Reflect on gratitude, then on your affirmations.

2. Close your eyes. Go to your Favorite Place in your mind.

3. Open your eyes. If you have a concern, write it on a card front. On the back write, "In this moment, this concern is handled," and put it in the outside pocket.

4. Close your eyes. Return to your Favorite Place. Ask, "What do I want?"

5. Open your eyes. Write your desire on a card front. On the back write, "Thank you for this gift."

Now we will go through each step one by one, so that you will have a thorough understanding of the complete process.

1. Get comfortable.

Set a gentle timer for twenty minutes, if you feel you need it (as I do.) Take out your Youthfulness Collage and place it where you can easily see it. You want to be relaxed and alert. Spend a few moments gazing at your collage and reflecting upon something that you are grateful for. Stay with it until the feeling of gratitude fills your mind. Then take out your affirmation cards. Say each one three times: out loud, whispering it, then saying it mentally.

2. Go to your Favorite Place in your mind.

Now that you've started to settle in, get ready – you're going on a trip! Take a moment and think about your favorite place on earth. Close your eyes and actually go there in your mind. It can be somewhere you've been before, or somewhere you've always wanted to go, or even a fantasy place. The most important component is that when you think of this place, you feel fresh and alive. **There is only eternal youth here.**

What does this place look like? If it's a quiet lake near a cabin in the mountains, use your mind to see the ripples that shimmer across the lake when the wind blows. What time of year is it? Is that a cool breeze with the scent of spring flowers? How do you feel here? Are you happy, quiet, excited, sexy, peaceful, in love?

Perhaps it's a café on the sidewalk in Paris as the sun is

rising. The warm smell of cappuccino with just the right froth tickles your nose. Lift the cup to your lips and taste the strong, slightly bitter brew that sends a brief jolt of good morning through your slowly-waking body.

This is your place where you are in love with you. Wherever it is that you love to be, go there now. The key is to feel all the sensations of actually being there right now and experiencing those feelings in this moment.

3. Deal with a concern if you have one.

Gently allow yourself to come back to the place your physical body inhabits, and slowly open your eyes. If a daily-living concern is there in the front of your mind, take out a file card and write down that concern in a simple sentence or phrase. If more than one comes to mind, write another card. If none come, great! Keep this simple and easy. The Creation Planning Exercises allow a new, fresh you to arise – the you that has always been there. However, if your experience of you is filled with creations and thoughts from the past, it is important to acknowledge those creations without judgment. Even though this process is *not* for taking care of everyday situations and circumstances, nor for finding a better way to take care of those everyday things, you need to acknowledge that your mind is filled with those past creations and that you spend many waking moments thinking about them.

The primary purpose of the Creation Planning Exercises is to reach that inner fountain of youth, but it is difficult to shift gears away from everyday concerns without acknowledging that we created them. That's why you are now creating a place where those thoughts can be recognized without making them wrong for appearing.

Turn over the "concern" card and on the back write, "In this moment, this concern is handled." The key phrase to this step is "in this moment." In this moment, whatever concerns you have about other areas of your life are set aside. As you write on the back of the card, recognize that you are giving yourself the gift of freedom – freedom from the thought, "I have to do something now to take care of the everyday affairs of my life." By making the commitment to work with your Creation Planner™, you are creating your life so that you have this time – this twenty minutes – available to you.

Take the card and place it in the outside pocket of your Creation Planner™. Leave it there. We will address the concern cards later in "Once-a-Week Creation Planning Exercises."

4. Ask, "What do I want?"

Close your eyes again and gently return to your favorite place. Touch something that you see there. If you're at the lake, dip your toe in the water. If you're in Paris, pick up that cup of cappuccino and take another sip. If you're out walking in nature, bend over and pick a flower. Lift it up to your nose and breathe in the beautiful fragrance. Take a moment to simply be there, without any action or agenda.

Now ask yourself this question: What do I want? Then return to being silent. Simply be there. Allow the response to arise in your awareness. The key to this is allowing and being silent. There's no need to make an effort to find an answer. The answer is always there; your job is to be still enough to recognize it.

Allow whatever arises to arise. It may be a crystal-clear statement or it may not make any sense at all to your mind. Simply receive it. The words or pictures that may arise are valuable, but the most important component is the *feeling* of that desire. For example, if the words "I want to be sexy and alive" came to you, notice what it is that being sexy and alive *feels* like!

One single caveat. Just suppose that while you're sitting in silence, waiting for your desire to arrive in your mind, a thought comes that has nothing to do with growing younger, nothing to do with a desire – but it's something you need to remember and write down right now, this very minute. Do it! Just go ahead and do it.

I'm reminded to tell you this because of what happened to me late last night. I was sitting in meditation, my mind was still and I was just blissfully allowing a desire to arise. Suddenly a long-forgotten memory plunged into my mind, and with it a whole paragraph for the bio of my book and website. (I mean *plunged!* It didn't just dribble in a little at a time.) Hey, I thought, I ought to use this. I fidgeted a little until I felt impelled to write it down. So I blew out the candles on my altar and ran down two flights of stairs, Colitta panting at my heels and wondering what in the world was going on at this crazy hour of the night. I typed it into the manuscript of this book; you can find it on the last page.

What's the reason for this story? No part of the ritual should feel so restricting that you cannot make changes that are necessary for you. You be the judge at all times of what feels right for you. When it *does* feel right, it most likely is Spirit bringing you inspiration. Sometimes inspiration comes in soft, barely audible internal whispers, and sometimes Spirit clobbers you over the head with a fantastic idea you can't ignore.

5. Write down your desire.

All right. You're sitting in your special place and a desire has arisen, along with the delicious feeling of its fulfillment. Slowly open your eyes and feel your body sitting on the chair. Wiggle your toes and fingers. Take another 3" x 5" card and write your desire on it (a simple phrase or sentence works most easily).

Sometimes what we desire is related to a concern we have. For example, if your desire reads, "I want to have a fresh, wrinkle-free face," underneath there is a concern, "I wish my wrinkles would go away." This is natural, but notice that your desire is addressing something you don't want. (Usually we are concerned about things we wish were different.) Rephrase your desire. If you have a word like "wrinkles" in your desire, the Law of Attraction will bring you more wrinkles. If your desire reads, "I want to lose weight," you are focusing on weight and the Law of Attraction will bring you more. Change the wording of your desire if it appears to focus on what you do *not* want. For example, in the first instance, you can reword your desire to "I want a fresh, young face." In the second instance, you might rephrase your desire to "I want a slim, beautiful body." The way you address what you want is vitally important. If you want more energy and vitality, instead of "I want to get rid of this tired and old feeling," write, "I want enormous energy and vitality, and I want to feel joyful!" **Always address what you want, rather than what you don't want, so your instructions to the Universe are clear.**

Look at what you've written, then turn the card over and write on the back, "Thank you for this gift," and place the card in the sleeve labeled "Creations." Take a moment again with your Youthfulness Collage, then fold it and place it inside the Creation Planner™. Zip up your Creation Planner™, blow out the candles and head off to the next part of your day.

Once-a-Week Creation Planning Exercises

You'll want to give yourself a little extra time to review your concern cards and desire cards once a week. Take the concern cards from the outside pocket of your Creation Planner™ and briefly review each. If a concern is no longer relevant, toss it. If it is still something concerning your present life, read the back of the card once more and replace it in the outside pocket.

Take your desire cards out of the sleeve labeled Creations. For each desire card, take out a fresh new 3" x 5" card. Use what is written on the desire card to create a new affirmation card. The purpose of the new card is to turn your desire into an affirmation that you say every day.

Notice that your desire cards are written in terms of "I want." Those cards cannot be used as daily affirmations because of the wording. If you say, "I want this or that," you are affirming that in this moment, you do not have what you want. Because your instructions to the Universe are that you *want* it, the Law of Attraction will continue to bring you the condition of wanting to have what you are asking for, but it will not bring you the desired object. Wanting expresses lack, a separation between you and something you do not have; desire is the magnetic *connection* between you and the object of your desire.

In order to give clear instructions to the Universe (or Spirit, or God), on the new card rephrase your desire into the present tense. For example:

- "I want a fresh, young face" becomes "I have a fresh, young face" on your affirmation card.

- "I want a slim, beautiful body" becomes "I am slim and beautiful."

- "I want enormous energy and vitality and I want to feel joyful" becomes, "I have enormous energy and vitality and I am joyful!"

There are no hard and fast rules about what you may affirm in your Creation Planning Exercises. If you want to affirm abundance, go right ahead. My favorite money affirmation is, "Money is constantly flowing into my life in avalanches of abundance for my personal use from expected and unexpected sources."

Discard your desire cards after they have been changed into affirmations. Put your new affirmation cards in the Affirmations sleeve and use them as part of the Creation Planning Exercises each day. From time to time review your affirmation cards and remove any that are no longer relevant for you.

Continue to use the Grow Younger tools on a regular basis. The 30-Second Grow Younger Method™ allows you to examine any old thought patterns that might still be present that are in conflict with what you asked for. It also helps reverse the aging limitations that have been implanted in your mind by generations of conditioning. Then reinforcing your new mindset with the Youthfulness Collage and Creation Planner™ opens the door for you to receive your desire.

SIX
HABITS TO
GUARANTEE
YOUR
SUCCESS

"Until one is committed, there is hesitancy,
the chance to draw back, always ineffectiveness.
Concerning all acts of initiative (and creation), there
is one elementary truth, the ignorance of which kills
countless ideas and splendid plans: that the moment
one definitely commits oneself, then Providence moves
too. All sorts of things occur to help one that would
never otherwise have occurred. A whole stream of
events issues from the decision, raising in one's favor
all manner of unforeseen incidents and meetings and
material assistance, which no man could have dreamed
would have come his way."

W. H. Murray, *The Scottish Himalayan Expedition*

You've learned the step-by-step 30-Second Grow Younger Method™ and you're devoting twenty minutes a day to the Creation Planning Exercises. Sure, you miss a day here or there. Everybody does. How do you prevent that missed day from stretching into a week? How can you be sure that you're on track, moving forward, and making the best use of your time and energy?

In addition to mastering the tools I've presented, there are six things you'll need to make it all happen. Five of them are habits of mind. The sixth requires that you engage your body to guarantee your success. These are assets you already possess, to one degree or another, and they'll be your stalwart companions. Nothing is impossible with friends like these. We'll go over each of them in order.

They are:
- Desire
- Clarity
- Attitude
- Belief
- Commitment
- Action

1. Desire

You need to be absolutely sure that you want to feel younger, be younger and act younger. You cannot be wishy-washy about it. If you half-heartedly decide to try this method, it will not work. True desire comes from your Higher Self. It's part of the expansion of the Universe – creating and manifesting and contributing to the Whole. If youthfulness is a true desire of your Higher Self, you will know it by how it makes you feel. If the thought of being youthful and having all the advantages that youthfulness brings gives you great joy, then you will benefit from the techniques in this book. However, if becoming young is not a true desire from your Higher Self, it will take effort to sustain the desire and eventually it will wither, tremendous doubts will set in, and you will get tired and lose interest in practicing the techniques. True desire needs no effort. The desire simply arises as a passion. Feel that passion with all the joyful emotion it generates.

Does this mean that, on those days you can't muster much enthusiasm for this or anything else – those days the glass isn't half-empty, it's downright dry – you'll lose the benefit of all the work you've put in? No, it doesn't. The 30-Second Grow Younger Method™ is sound; keep using it. Do your affirmations and give your Creation Planning Exercises the best shot you can. You may find that doing these things will lift you out of that dismal spot. Trust in the techniques to bring about a younger you. The stronger your desire, the easier it is for your subconscious mind to align itself with this goal.

2. Clarity

A clear vision of a younger you is essential. The vision must be specific and palpable and you should engage as many senses as possible in designing your vision. Your Youthfulness Collage will help provide this vision. Do not be concerned about *how* your desire to grow younger will come about – that's the job of the Universe. Your job is to provide a clear mental picture for your subconscious mind to focus on. The Law of Attraction will magnetize what you need to make it happen.

3. Attitude

You need to feel upbeat and positive that you can make these changes happen. You need to love the idea of being younger; of having a sharp, clear mind; of developing relationships which nurture you and allow you to nurture others. Most of all, you need to make it *fun*!

4. Belief

Know in your heart of hearts that you are growing younger. Believe totally in the Universe's ability to make it happen. When doubt creeps in, recognize it as a vestige of your old mindset and gently escort it out. Have faith in your inner ability to choose what's best for yourself and to follow through on that conviction. Even if you cannot yet see or feel the results on the outside, keep reminding yourself that growing younger begins on the inside and it *is* happening.

5. Commitment

It is a law of the Universe that when you make a commitment to a goal, the Universe will do everything to make it happen for you. Declare your commitment to become younger and then be aware of people, situations and circumstances the Universe is bringing to you that will help you reach your goal. This is part of the ancient secret that people in the "know" have practiced for millennia. In translating Goethe, John Anster has given us the now famous quote: "Whatever you can do, or dream you can, begin it. Boldness has genius, power, and magic in it." Do not be deterred. Surround yourself with others who will reaffirm your commitment to your goal.

6. Action

Doing should be a natural form of action, and should not replace *being*. When you've visualized what you want to *be* and you are prompted to take action, the action will be effortless. Do not strain or push yourself; that will set you back and make your mind focus on what you do not want. Just keep your intention to grow younger gently on your mind and love yourself as you are.

Be alert to the clues the Universe is sending you regarding fulfillment of your desire to grow younger. Those signs can come in any form. Watch for them, listen for them. It might be someone talking on TV or radio. You might hear a friend or family member say something relevant. You might read something in a book. A clue might come through during your meditation.

Whatever the source, be ready to act on appropriate opportunities. Don't find yourself in the position of the very religious man whose home was in the path of a flood when a dam broke. As word spread throughout the valley below, people hurried to save themselves. But this man refused to leave his house. "God will take care of me," he said. Just before the flood waters reached his house, his neighbors urged him to hop into their waiting car and flee, but he stayed put. When the water began to fill his house, he climbed onto the roof. Soon a young man in a boat rowed by and urged him to jump in. "No," the man replied. "God will take care of me." So he stuck to his roof and the boat headed off. Finally, as the waters began to lap at the top of the roof, a helicopter approached, and a rope was lowered. "Grab on and we'll haul you up," the pilot shouted. But the man refused. "God will take care of me," he said. Finally, the flood covered the house and as the man began swimming madly to stay afloat, he cried out to God, "Why didn't you save me?" A voice from heaven answered, "I sent you a car, a boat and a helicopter. What more do you want?"

God helps those who allow God to help. Spirit provides the clues, opportunities and inspiration. It's up to you to take action by putting into practice the age-reversing steps Spirit prompts you to take, including the techniques in this book.

How Long Will It Take and What Will It Look Like?

How long will it take for youthfulness to show up as a physical manifestation in this realm of experience? That depends on you. How strongly do you believe it is happening? How clear are you in your vision? How single-minded are you in this vision? Is it possible you are entertaining thoughts that are contrary to your vision of a younger you? How aware are you of the clues the Universe is sending to help fulfill your desire? Are you cultivating present-moment awareness so that you are as open as possible to the people, situations and circumstances the Universe is sending to help you grow younger? Those clues happen only in the present moment, so if your thoughts are dwelling on the past or on a future that is at odds with a younger you, you cannot receive the clues that absolutely, positively, definitely come to assist you in fulfilling this desire. Through the Law of Attraction, it could all happen in an instant, but because our conditioning says we grow old, not young, the manifestation of a younger you requires patience. You cannot force it to happen; that will only slow you down. And demonstrating impatience puts you in a position of *wanting*, which is contrary to *desire*, and that will slow you down even more.

The tool of setting deadlines is a process many of us have

used successfully in our careers. It is not a useful tool for the process of growing younger. (And that is besides the fact that it is a "dead"line.) Setting a deadline in business or a profession is designed to force an outcome, which is the opposite of allowing the Universe to bring what we desire. A deadline to the Universe brings in fear and doubt of the Universe's capability to bring your desire into manifestation in the perfect manner. In addition, a deadline makes detachment to the outcome difficult. What you're doing is putting it into the linear timeframe of the human mind and that can take it out of the realm of *now*, which is the realm in which the Universe works.

Now here's the hardest part: **Don't try to dictate exactly what your desire should look like when it appears in your "real" life.** That is the job of the Universe. Be specific about your desire but be detached from the outcome. This is not a contradiction. You need to let the Universe know exactly what you want, but the Universe might have something even better for you, a way of fulfilling your desire that you couldn't even possibly imagine.

By being detached, you are demonstrating certainty that what you desire will appear. Giving your desire to the Universe and having no anxiety about whether or how it will arrive has to do with *who* is making it happen. With total trust in the Creator of All, or the Universe, you can relax regarding the results.

When Action Becomes Habit

As you begin to practice the techniques for growing younger, you'll find it necessary to reinforce those techniques daily until they become habit and are an automatic part of your behavior. I learned this approach from a master, Bob Swanick, owner of Fairmont, a bank consulting company headquartered in Frederick, PA. I am privileged to be part of Fairmont on a post-retirement basis after fifteen years working with clients. Fairmont is, in my mind, the best company in the world and Bob Swanick is the best boss in the world.

Fairmont's expertise is in providing its bank clients with a proven method for changing order-takers into salespeople. This process for changing behavior includes training, but training alone – even training coupled with goals and incentives – is ineffective unless each set of skills is reinforced day by day and transferred into behaviors used consistently with the customer. Without strong, persistent reinforcement of the skills, drilling them over and over and over again until they become "muscle memory", the skills would be gone two weeks after training.

I tell you this because I don't want your skills to be gone two weeks after reading this book. When you start something new, it takes persistent practice to change the grooves in your brain from the old pattern to the new pattern. *Changing the grooves in your brain* is the terminology I use to remind myself that whenever we learn something new, whenever we practice new positive thoughts, our brains continue to develop. Science has proven this. You're never too old to make positive changes in your life.

Can you think of a time when you learned to do something new? I can. I had been driving a car with the gear shift on the steering wheel and when I bought a new car, one with the gear shift on the floor, my hand would automatically rise to the steering wheel when I needed to shift. Grooves had been worn in my brain from constant, repetitive shifting at the steering wheel. It took conscious effort and practice to form new grooves in my brain. Only then would my hand automatically go to the gear shift on the floor. The same methodology applies to observing your thoughts.

A New Idea Became a Life-Changing Habit

One of the most important days of my life was the day I learned to meditate. It was 1974, and I had heard that Transcendental Meditation, as taught by Maharishi Mahesh Yogi, was being conducted in Morristown, NJ. Those were the days when our family of six didn't have two nickels to rub together. Our home business hit a rocky bottom, bill collectors were a daily torment, and it was an emotional struggle to use some of the meager funds we had for the meditation class fee.

Somehow, though, I knew that I just had to go – and I'm so glad I did. When I began to meditate, it felt like coming home. The whole experience was so powerful for me I wept the first several times. The gift I received that day sent ripples throughout my life. My young children benefited from a more peaceful mother, my insomnia disappeared, and with the calm confidence meditation lent me, I was able to find a job that grew into a wonderful, successful career.

Today, meditation is not only a fulfilling personal habit, it's a lifestyle choice that I enjoy and love. I live in northern New Mexico in a house with a meditation room at the top, in a neighborhood of people who are kind, fun, and warm-hearted. Around here, if you borrow a stick of butter, your neighbors won't ask for it back; they might need something different next time they run out. I haven't found anyone yet from whom I can borrow a jigger of Laphroaig Scotch, but I'm not counting out the possibility. There are plenty of other neighbors here besides those who belong to the nearby Tibetan Buddhist Center.

Truthfully, I'm delighted to be living so close – within walking distance! – of the Buddhist Center. I've had the chance to attend retreats at the center and I am especially fond of Yongey Mingyur Rinpoche, a visiting lama who is less than half my age but is wise and spiritually very powerful. Whether he's teaching an ancient text at the center or laughing over tea at my house, I've found him to be an enlightened spiritual teacher like no other.

Rinpoche doesn't seem to mind that my ideas and influences extend beyond the reach of traditional Buddhism. The Buddhist precepts are close to my heart, but I love just as well the adventurous spirit of Auntie Mame's philosophy: "Life is a banquet," she says, "and most poor suckers are starving to death." When Patrick Dennis wrote the book *Auntie Mame*, a fictional account of his good-natured, fun-loving aunt who was never afraid to try a new experience and who believed in keeping an open mind about everything and everybody, he couldn't have known what an impact her example would have on me.

So – half serious, half tongue-in-cheek – I call myself an "Auntie Mame Buddhist". I steer clear of calling it a label, though. The sticky stuff on the back of a label doesn't adhere well to me, and I'm happy to keep it that way.

Gathering Inspiration

Inspired ideas, when put into practice, can create a whole new living reality. In addition to receiving creative insights during meditation, I've been inspired by the teaching and writing of others. You'll find a number of valuable references listed in Recommended Reading in the back of this book, but I want to honor a few of the books that, over the years, have made the greatest impact on me.

When I was about nine, my mother gave me my first

Edgar Cayce book, and from that point on, I was hooked on metaphysics. I read *Mystic Path to Cosmic Power* by Vernon Howard in 1967, and that book became my constant companion throughout my thirties and forties. The message of awakening, of becoming aware of our thoughts and trusting in a Higher Self, all made so much sense to me. But it was more than that. It was not just a mental agreement with the words I read. The message resonated inside me. It rang true. That's how it is with all the spiritual books I read: I assimilate into my consciousness whatever rings true.

In the 1980s, the *Seth* books by Jane Roberts, most especially *The Nature of Personal Reality*, powerfully reinforced my efforts to observe my thoughts and take inspired action. They taught me to actually correlate my thoughts with what manifested in my life, both positive and negative.

Books, as well as people, situations and circumstances you encounter, may all offer opportunities to take action with various techniques. Make use of the Law of Attraction to magnetize the ones that will do you the most good. Keep in mind, too, that taking care of your body, mind and spirit, and your relationships are all part of the process of growing younger. For suggestions regarding that process, I strongly recommend that you read *Grow Younger, Live Longer* by Deepak Chopra, MD and David Simon, MD, and *Life Beyond 100: Secrets of the Fountain of Youth* by Norm Shealy, MD, PhD.

I look forward to offering a comprehensive program of twenty-one age-reversing steps to a more joyful life in my next book. Check my website *www.howtogrowyounger.com* for details.

WHY GROWING YOUNGER MATTERS

"Our deepest fear is not that we are inadequate. Our deepest fear is that we are powerful beyond measure. It is our light, not our darkness that most frightens us. We ask ourselves, 'Who am I to be brilliant, gorgeous, talented, fabulous?' Actually, who are you not to be?

"You are a child of God. Your playing small doesn't serve the world. There's nothing enlightened about shrinking so that people won't feel insecure around you. We are meant to shine, as children do. We were born to make manifest the glory of God that is within us. It's not just in some of us; it's in everyone. And as we let our own light shine, we unconsciously give other people permission to do the same. As we're liberated from our own fear, our presence automatically liberates others."

Marianne Williamson, *A Return to Love*

Since you've come this far, you know this book is not intended to glorify youthful appearance in order to get you admiring glances and have you become the role model of everyone in your age group. Don't be surprised if you do! This book will help you glow with a youthful radiance that comes from the light within, but that glow will do more for you than garner compliments. It will help you achieve your greater mission to assist all those around you.

The Secret Method for Growing Younger invites you to grow beyond the individual into the group consciousness. To do that, it is absolutely essential that you, as an individual, learn to shine and be *who you truly are.* That, in itself, is your most significant contribution to the world.

Imagine Earth transformed into a planet that honors and respects the carriers of wisdom and seeks solutions *from* its elders, not just *for* its elders. This paradigm shift, based on individual transformation and the collective quantum leap of humanity, is the point of this book.

We are all connected – my emotions affect your emotions, scientists tell us, and yours affect mine. I've heard it said that the air we breathe was once in the lungs of Jesus and Buddha and Mohammed, and yes, Marilyn Monroe, according to science. The mystics and sages tell us that psychic energy interpenetrates all of us. Everything we do individually affects humanity as a whole. By being whole and youthful yourself, you help the world around you to fully express its wholeness and youthfulness

The Uniqueness of Baby Boomers

Every generation has had the same expectations, the same mental images of what it means to be old. Each generation has reinforced those mental images and passed them along to the next. If we were to continue to harbor inherited images of aging, we would magnetize more of the same of what has always been expected for millennia for elders. But we have the opportunity to do it differently.

It is not surprising that this movement to grow younger should be happening right now. With the baby-boomer generation peeking over the crest of midlife, a growing number of you are wondering how to put your distinctive spin on the process of maturing. As a group, you mix a deep interest in personal and spiritual growth with a willingness to see things from a different perspective. More so than previous generations, you are savvy about your choices and not willing to settle for less than you deserve. That same openness which challenged social conventions around civil rights and gender equality is ripe to replace the "old" way of aging with the revolution in youthfulness that is charted for you in this book. Imagine the tremendous impact of your collective power working with the Law of Attraction to create a whole new world!

Your Gift to the World

The Law of Attraction never fails. Everything is possible if you focus and practice. Think about the contribution you can make to mankind by consciously changing your mindset and your expectations for your later years. Think about what can happen when you use the Law of Attraction and attract people, situations and circumstances that bring you age-reversing solutions. Consider the result of your then taking action and utilizing those solutions to grow younger. **You will grow younger.**

When it's working for you, it would be very surprising if you don't feel as I do: I want to run around and tell everyone how powerful and great it feels to actually be younger than I was before. I want everyone to feel as fresh and alive and youthful as I do. I want to shout, "Cancel, cancel," whenever I hear someone say, "I'm getting old." Or, "At my age, who knows if I'll be alive next year." Or, "My old bones can't take this cold." Or any of a myriad of catchphrases that reinforce the old mindset and continue to bolster expectations of mental and physical decline as we age, for generation after generation after generation.

You have the ability to create a shift in society – to increase the consciousness of humanity. Each of us can do our part by being aware of our thoughts and our words and by using the Law of Attraction to bring us the joy of youthfulness. It is up to us. We need to individually change ourselves, and then, together, help change the consciousness of America and the rest of the planet. It is not up to the younger generations to do this for us. We need to do it for ourselves.

Attitudes Towards Elders

Some nations honor their elders, but America is not one of them. Here in the United States our society glorifies youth and has an aversion to old age. We loathe growing old and often show that loathing in the way we treat our older citizens. Some other societies link age with wisdom, experience and distinction – they reserve a special status for people who have lived a long time on the Earth.

But here in the United States you can see the attitude towards older Americans. In business it's rare for older people to be considered strong, clear-thinking leaders and many of us are encouraged to retire when we reach a certain age. We're often portrayed on TV and in films as inept and silly.

There are a lot of us. The number of people 65 years and older will double in the next thirty years in the United States. It is a crisis that government sees brewing, the question of how to take care of all of us. Businesses are churning out products and drugs to take advantage of the commercial opportunities they see both now and on the horizon for this demographic.

The expectation of government is that we will be in poor

health, we will wither, we will have unclear minds – and *then* what will they do with us? The concern of government focuses on a predicted increase in the demand for healthcare and social services. There is no vision of us as a valuable resource. What if government, instead of expecting that it needs to provide *for* many of us, could expect to get valuable insights and wisdom *from* many of us? That could happen with the massive turnaround that we foster.

We need to change the expectation in ourselves first. And then we need to spread it to our neighborhoods, our towns, our state, our nation. When our expectations for ourselves change – and our success influences others to change – our society will have to change. Government programs and policies for the collective good of its older citizens need to be designed with the assistance of more older persons with raised consciousness.

Living Younger Now

Over the years, many of us have lived this trademark of modern life, this practice we have of stretching twenty-four hours into a container big enough to hold a day and a half's activity. America leads the world when it comes to overworking and underrelaxing. But those of us who have finished fulfilling our household duties are ready for a different challenge, now.

We have more time right now than the younger

generations. That can mean more time to meditate and contemplate, or it can mean hours in front of the TV. The funny thing is, when you begin to focus and practice the age-reversing techniques, listening for Spirit's guidance and enjoying being alive, television begins to lose its appeal.

I don't spurn modern media or conveniences. I watch *Oprah* while I'm on the treadmill in the afternoon when it's Colitta's time to eat. Sometimes in the evening I watch *Larry King* (if it's upbeat and positive), *America's Funniest Home Movies* or *Comedy Central* – something to get me laughing. And occasionally I watch a movie.

But I rarely watch the news anymore. This came about unexpectedly, when – several years ago – my copy of *Time* magazine stopped coming. My subscription hadn't expired and I never received a renewal notice of any kind since; it just stopped showing up in the mailbox. I decided to just let it go and started listening to NPR's news on the radio each morning. A few days later, my radio broke! That's when I realized: *Oh, I get it. The Universe is telling me not to spend so much time focusing on the news. It's not my job. It might be someone else's, but it's not* mine. My job is to listen to Spirit and take action based on the promptings I receive.

The time you free up by watching less TV you can use to join or create a group of like-minded people who also want to grow younger. You can encourage each other to live in the present and practice your age-reversing techniques together. Through the Law of Attraction methods provided in this book and others, you and your friends can learn to access that incredible fountain of joy deep inside you – that manifestation of Spirit. Then you and the others can spread the joy of youthfulness from mind to mind until a critical mass is reached and elders become empowered, valued members of society.

Reaching Critical Mass

Have you heard of the hundredth monkey syndrome? Ken Keyes, Jr. tells of the Japanese snow monkeys, or macaques, who were observed in the wild for over thirty years. The researchers, studying the colony on the island of Koshima, provided the macaques with sweet potatoes, dropping them on the sandy beaches. One juvenile decided her sweet potato would taste better without the sand and washed it. She taught her mother and her playmates this new technique. Over the next six years, other members of the colony gradually learned this new method, until finally, one morning, they reached critical mass. By that evening, all members of the colony were washing their sweet potatoes. Even more startling, macaques on the nearby islands and on the mainland also began washing their sweet potatoes at the same time, never having come into contact with the Koshima macaques. This means that when just one more person tunes in to a new behavior, it can tip the scales and create critical mass. When critical mass is achieved, the new behavior may be communicated easily from mind to mind.

When you feel fresh and new and alive with the wonderment and joy of creating and expressing yourself, your thoughts and emotions will affect those around you, and soon, those around you will want to know your secret. And then you will feel compelled to share your secret, as I am. Others will also be inspired to consciously change their mindsets and expectations, consciously creating the life they want.

A Shift is Happening

All those who are tuned in to the energies of the mind say a shift in consciousness is happening on our planet right now. Growing younger is part of this shift. We – those of us who are approaching or are in our retirement years – have the opportunity to become known as one of the planet's greatest assets. We can lead the way. We can help humanity make that paradigm shift. We can be the pivotal generation group bridging the old human way to the new. We, who are finished with diapers and term papers and working two jobs to provide for our families, can take the time and energy to create the shift to a new consciousness.

You have to be in good health, you have to have a clear mind, you need all your faculties present – but it takes an experienced life to come to this place. That's why it's the job for baby boomers. Yours is the generation that is pioneering this new frontier of transformation and renewal.

A New Possibility

Many of us have already been using the Law of Attraction, consciously or unconsciously, to be productive, valuable members of society. Been there, done that. Why do we want to be younger now? Do we simply desire to be twenty-five years old, or thirty-five years old, or whatever age, so we can go back and have more of life *as it was*? Do we want to again do everything we did at that age, only with a higher level of functionality than is traditionally expected in one's later years? Do we want younger minds and bodies so we can scuba dive, compete in the corporate or professional world, party all night or do whatever we enjoyed doing when our minds and bodies were in what society considered their prime?

We're raising the bar. What if we, this older generation, shift our consciousness to a youthful outlook, ripe with possibilities, ready for creative expression, an expression of something we can't even now imagine? What if we focus and practice being in the *now*, while envisioning all of humanity living lives that are empowered and grow better and better as the years progress, *without* telling Spirit exactly what that vision should look like? What if we leave some empty space for Spirit to deliver countless possibilities to enrich our lives and enrich the world we live in?

Could it be that **life beyond one hundred will be radically different, more wonderful, more empowering and more fun than we could possibly imagine in our wildest dreams**? Could it be that there is something waiting there for us to discover – something we don't even know about yet?

I pose those questions, but I don't have the answers. All I know right now is that I expect to live, *really* live, until I die. I plan to kick up my heels and dance at my great-grandchild's wedding and, when I'm 108, I expect to remember that a full house beats a flush and I will *still* be winning at poker. Come along with me.

Let's take this ride together.

Recommended Reading

Aitken, Robert. *Taking the Path of Zen.* San Francisco: North Point Press, 1982.

Alder, Very Stanley. *The Initiation of the World.* New York: Samuel Weiser, 1972.

Alder, Vera Stanley. *The Finding of the Third Eye.* New York: Samuel Weiser, 1968.

Arrien, Angeles, Ph.D. *The Four-Fold Way.* San Francisco: HarperSanFrancisco, 1993.

Blood, Casey, Ph.D. Science, *Sense and Soul.* Los Angeles: Renaissance Books, 2001.

Braden, Gregg. *The Isaiah Effect.* New York: Three Rivers Press, 2000.

Butler, Meryl Ann. "A Romp Through the Quantum Field with Gregg Braden and Dr. Bruce Lipton, Part 1 and 2." *Awareness* Magazine, September/October, 2006 and November/December, 2006.

Cayce, Edgar, There is a River. Virginia Beach, VA: A.R.E. Press, revised edition 1997

Childre, Doc. *Freeze Frame.* Boulder Creek, CA: Planetary Publications, 1998.

Childre, Doc. Martin, Howard. Beech, Donna. *The Heartmath® Solution.* San Francisco: HarperSanFrancisco, 2000.

Chopra, Deepak, M.D. *Ageless Body, Timeless Mind.* New York: Harmony Books, 1993.

Chopra, Deepak, M.D., Simon, David, M.D. *Grow Younger, Live Longer.* New York: Harmony Press, 2001.

Cota-Robles, Patricia D. *The Awakening… Eternal Youth, Vibrant Health, Radiant Beauty.* Tucson, AZ: New Age Study of Humanity's Purpose, Inc., 1993

Dennis, Patrick. *Auntie Mame.* New York: Broadway Books, 2001.

Dyer, Wayne W., M.D. *Manifest Your Destiny.* New York: Harper Perennial, 1997.

Dyer, Wayne W., M.D. *The Power of Intention.* Carlsbad, CA: Hay House, 2004.

Emmons, Robert A., McCullough, Michael E. *The Psychology of Gratitude.* New York: Oxford University Press, 2004.

Emoto, Masaru, Dr. *The Hidden Messages in Water.* New York: Atria, 2005.

Essene, Virginia, ed. *New Cells, New Bodies, New Life!* Santa Clara, CA: S.E.E. Publishing Company, 1991.

Gawain, Shakti. *Creative Visualization.* Novato, CA: Nataraj Publishing/New World Library, 2002.

Goleman, Daniel. *Social Intelligence: The New Science of Human Relationships.* New York: Bantam Books, 2006.

H.H. Dalai Lama, Tenzin Gyatso. *Path to Bliss: A Practical Guide to Stages of Meditation*. Ithaca, NY: Snow Lion Publications, 1991.

Hicks, Esther, Hicks, Jerry. *Ask and It Is Given*. Carlsbad, CA: Hay House, Inc., 2004.

Howard, Vernon. *The Mystic Path to Cosmic Power*. West Nyack, NY: Parker Publishing Company, 1967.

Kamm, Laura Alden. *Intuitive Wellness*™. New York: Atria Books, 2006.

Kamm, Laura Alden. *A Step-By-Step Guide to Intuitive Wellness*™. Scottsdale, AZ: Mayflower Press, 2000.

Kelder, Peter. *Ancient Secret of the Fountain of Youth*™ *Book 2*. New York: Doubleday, 1998.

Keyes, Ken, Jr. *Handbook to Higher Consciousness*. Berkeley, CA: Living Love Center, 1975.

Keyes, Ken, Jr. *The Hundredth Monkey*. Marina del Rey: DeVorss & Company, 1984.

Lipton, Bruce H., Ph.D. *The Biology of Belief: Unleashing the Power of Consciousness, Matter and Miracles*. Santa Rosa, CA: Mountain of Love/Elite Books, 2005.

Maharaj, Sri Nisargadatta, Frydman, Maurice. *I Am That*. Durham, NC: The Acorn Press, 1973.

Moore, Thomas. *Care of the Soul: A Guide for Cultivating Depth and Sacredness in Everyday Life*. New York: HarperCollins, 1992.

Nhat Hanh, Thich. *The Miracle of Mindfulness.* Boston: Beacon Press, 1976.

Ouspensky, P.D. *In Search of the Miraculous.* New York: Harcourt, Brace & World, 1949.

Page, Christine, M.D. *Frontiers of Health: How to Heal the Whole Person.* London: Ryder, 2000.

Pearsall, Paul, Ph.D. *The Heart's Code: Tapping the Wisdom and Power of Our Heart Energy.* New York: Broadway Books, 1998.

Revel, Jean-François. Matthieu Ricard. *The Monk and the Philosopher.* New York: Schocken Books, 1998.

Roberts, Jane. *The Nature of Personal Reality: Specific, Practical Techniques for Solving Everyday Problems and Enriching the Life You Know.* Novato, CA: New World Library, 1994.

Saint-Marie, Mary/Sheoekah. *The Holy Sight.* Mount Shasta, CA: Ancient Beauty Studio, 2004.

Shealy, C. Norman, M.D. *Life beyond 100.* New York: Jeremy P. Tarcher/Penguin, 2005.

Spalding, Baird T. *Life and Teaching of the Masters of the Far East, Vol. 1.* Marina del Rey, CA: DeVorss & Co., 1964.

Teilhard de Chardin, Pierre. *Building the Earth.* New York: Avon Books, 1965.

Teilhard de Chardin, Pierre. *The Phenomenon of Man.* New York: Harper & Row, 1959.

Thetford, William, Dr., Schucman, Helen, Dr. *A Course in Miracles*. New York: Foundation for Inner Peace, 1975.

Tolle, Eckhart. *Practicing the Power of Now*. Novato, CA: New World Library, 1999.

Tolle, Eckhart. *The Power of Now*. Novato, CA: New World Library, 1999.

Torassa, Ulysses. "Living Long and Prospering". San Francisco Chronicle, 3 June, 2001.

Trungpa, Chögyam. *The Myth of Freedom and the Way of Meditation*. Boulder, CO: Shambhala, 1976.

Walsch, Neale Donald. *Conversations with God: An Uncommon Dialogue, Book 1*. New York: G.P. Putnam's Sons, 1995.

Wilber, Ken. *The Marriage of Sense and Soul*. New York: Broadway Books, 1998.

Williamson, Marianne. *A Return to Love*. New York: HarperCollins, 1992.

Yogananda, Paramahansa. *Autobiography of a Yogi*. Los Angeles: Self-Realization Fellowship, 1993.

ACKNOWLEDGEMENTS

This book is not just a program of techniques for growing younger. It is also a story of my personal journey of experiences with the *Law of Attraction*, both before I knew there was a Universal Law that governed everything that shaped my life, and after I consciously used this Law to make my life what I wanted it to be.

I did not take this personal journey alone. There are so many people who have touched my life and become a part of me – people like Nicholas and Anna Bilansky, my parents, and my children, Peter, Summer, Winton and Harper, whose touch permeated my entire being and blessed me with the strength and encouragement to live my dreams and make this book a real, physical object you can hold in your hand and assimilate into your mind.

My grandchildren, Rhianna Ahola, Genevieve and Siri Wood, Tetsuro, Kan and Yohta Namba, Lilya Pocock Wood, and Sam Petty have made indelible marks on my heartstrings as have my stepchildren, Michel and Danielle Duvoisin; my foster daughters, Elaine Eib and Uma Devi; and my sister, Helen Gallant, and brother, Joe Bilansky.

There are those whose touch tickled my being with the effervescence of their tender friendships, including Pintki and John Murray, Dolores Zukoski, Linda Duvoisin, Joan Sleight

Thompson, Suzanne Bell, Mike Bradford, Helice Rose and Michael Walsh, Steve McElmury, Don Larsen and yes, the Pottsville High School Class of 1954.

My career was a huge success thanks to my former boss, Dick Schaub, who gave me the opportunity to express outrageous marketing ideas for the bank, and to those in our in-house ad agency who did the work and gave me the credit, especially Marie Koch and Gail Colella. Later, at Fairmont I had so much fun and made so much money, thanks to my boss, Bob Swanick, and my colleagues and clients, especially Affinity Federal Credit Union.

This book, too, has its own life, touched by those who helped birth it. I thank Summer for being my angel of compassion, my pillar of strength and encouragement, and for using her extraordinary talents to organize and format my untidy heap of writings, as well as help write and edit. I am very grateful to Peter for leaving Kauai to spend the last three weeks with me wrapping up this book with last-minute writing and editing, and nurturing my spirit. Prior to that he gifted me with twice-a-day calls (and sometime more) to prompt, inspire, encourage, poke fun, make me laugh, hold me to my hours-of-writing commitment and share with me his ideas for perfecting the Creation Planner. I give many thanks to Dr. Norm Shealy for writing the Foreward and lending credence to an unknown writer with his outstanding reputation in the field of energy medicine. My great appreciation goes to Jeff Spicer for his brilliant design of this book, especially the chapter dolphins, to Allegra Huston, another one of my talented editors, and to Beth Sumner-Wichmann, whose steady assistance, attention to commas and kind heart kept me on track. And to Eve Konstantine and Pam Miller, who also helped collaborate with me in bringing this book and my website to fruition, I offer my deep gratitude.

Last, but not least, I am profoundly grateful to all the ascended masters, sages, and authors of ancient and current texts on youthfulness and the Law of Attraction for the inspiration that led to the development of *The Secret Method For Growing Younger.*

ABOUT THE AUTHOR

Ellen Wood is an award-winning bank marketing and advertising executive who has authored or been featured in over 30 articles in national magazines and newspapers, and has given numerous talks throughout the country.

Ellen began her career in the late 1950s as a radio journalist for WPAM in Pottsville, PA. In New York City during the early 1960s, she wrote and illustrated fashion industry publications and was a model with the Eva Burnay Model Agency.

Her lifelong interest in metaphysics includes over 40 years of research exploring Eastern spirituality and Western psychology; attending seminars, workshops and retreats; and practicing techniques for balancing and joyfully integrating body, mind and spirit.

During her entire eight years of grade school at St. John the Baptist, she received only two red marks (they're bad): one in the first grade for Religion and one in the sixth for Conduct. However, she won two Holy Pictures (they're good) for Reading in the third grade and was always chosen to be an angel in processions. (That's *really* good, especially after getting a red mark in Conduct.)

www.howtogrowyounger.com

Order Form
StarHouse Creations

To order copies of:

THE SECRET METHOD FOR GROWING YOUNGER - $11.95*+$3.49 S&H**

(for First Book)

$2.00 S&H

(for Each Additional Book)

Please fill out the form below and mail it with your check or money order to:

StarHouse Creations

PO Box 890

Questa, NM 87556

NAME _____

ADDRESS _____

CITY_____ STATE _____ ZIP_____

COUNTRY_____TELEPHONE_____

E-MAIL _____

*$1.00 from the sale of each book goes to charity

**Shipping & Handling

Add $2.00 for US Priority Mail

Add $4.00 for Global Priority to Canada & Mexico

Add $8.00 for all other countries

NUMBER OF COPIES _____ ORDER SUBTOTAL _____

S&H _____

NM residents add 6% sales tax _____

TOTAL _____

To pay with a credit card via PayPal®, visit: ***www.howtogrowyounger.com***